"This book offers much needed encouragement to families who are tired of hearing society's endless whine about the impossibility of mothers staying home to raise their own children. The fact is, it can be done, and it is being done, with ingenuity and good cheer. . . . Her Eleven Miserly Guidelines are completely practical and at the top of the list is the most important: 'Don't confuse frugality with depriving yourself.'"

—Ginny Silva
In a review for *Christian Parenting Today*

"Jonni McCoy shows great understanding in the power of living frugally. It can be done, and she can show you how, so if you want to take back control of your finances, start here."

—Pat Verretto
Frugal Living Guide at About.com

Miserly MOMS

Living on ONE Income in a TWO-Income Economy

JONNI McCOY

BETHANYHOUSE
MINNEAPOLIS, MINNESOTA

Published by Bethany House Publishers
A Ministry of Bethany Fellowship International
11400 Hampshire Avenue South
Bloomington, Minnesota 55438
www.bethanyhouse.com

Printed in the United States of America by
Bethany Press International, Bloomington, Minnesota 55438

Library of Congress Cataloging-in-Publication Data

McCoy, Jonni.
    Miserly moms : living on one income in a two-income economy / by
Jonni McCoy.—3rd ed.
       p.   cm.
Includes index.
    ISBN 0-7642-2612-6
    1. Consumer education. 2. Home economics—Accounting.
I. Title.
    TX335 .M384   2001
640—dc21   2001002727

I would like to dedicate this book
to my dear husband, Beau,
and to my children, Jeremy and Jessica.

To Beau, who provided such varied
types of support that made writing possible.
He also never failed in his belief that
I could write something of value.
He has always believed in me.
His suggestions were always on target.

It is through that encouragement
that I have become the woman of God
that I am today.

And to my children, who always inspire me
to be a better person.
And for their patience while I was working.

JONNI McCOY holds a Bachelor of Arts degree in Speech Communication from the University of California at Santa Barbara. Prior to motherhood, she spent ten years as a senior buyer and supervisor for electronics firms such as Apple Computer and National Semiconductor. She presents seminars on living for less to women's groups and other conferences. She has been practicing her frugal ways since 1991. Jonni has appeared on the *Gayle King Show* and *The 700 Club,* and radio programs such as *Family Life Today* and the *Dick Staub Show.* She has also been featured in *Good Housekeeping* and *Woman's Day* magazines. Jonni and her husband, Beau, make their home in Colorado Springs, Colorado, where they homeschool their children.

Miserly MOMS

$ $ $

For more help with saving money,
visit our Web site.

We offer numerous resources for
the frugal person
(or frugal wanna-be).
There are articles,
links to other money-saving sites,
discussion groups,
and much more!
Drop by soon!

WWW.MISERLYMOMS.COM

ACKNOWLEDGMENTS

*I would like to thank Kat and Craig Osten
for the many hours they invested in reading this book.
Your ideas made it even better!*

CONTENTS

Why This Book Is Different

*W*hen I first wrote this book, our family lived in one of the most expensive parts of America—the San Francisco Bay Area. Most families were spending half their income to pay the high rent or mortgage. Consequently, most families needed both parents to work, just to get by. We were one of those families. According to statistics, my husband and I were a middle-income family, with my job providing half of our joint income. I was a career woman who received much joy from her work.

After our first child was born, I began to feel God tugging at my heart to stay home to raise our family. At first I thought I hadn't heard correctly. We couldn't live in this area on half of our joint income. At least that's what we believed. Trying to interpret what God was saying to me, I arranged a job-sharing program where I worked part time. We continued in that lifestyle for several years. Once it became clear that the part-time arrangement was not God's plan, and that I was supposed to stay home full time, we were back to square one.

We thought we would have to move to a less expensive community in order to live on my husband's salary alone. So that's what we decided to do, but things changed at the last minute. We made an offer on a house, and someone made an offer on our home. One night I realized that I didn't want my husband commuting two to three hours each day, and I didn't like the idea of being so far away from our church and our friends. So we got out of both house offers with no penalties. But I had already quit my job. So there we were, living on half of our income in an expensive area.

Our choices were either for me to go back to work or to somehow reduce our expenses. I knew I was supposed to stay at home with my family. So instead of bringing in a salary, I began to research how we could make our money go further. This opened my eyes to the hidden costs in the way we lived, and I questioned whether some people could even afford to be working.

When we calculated what our loss of income would do to our budget, we didn't realize how many hidden costs would disappear once I stopped working. Given the cost of day care, taxes, gasoline, parking, convenience foods (we were often too tired to cook after work), lunches out, office clothes, and all the other amenities associated with working, not much of our salaries were even used at home. I wasn't alone in this realization. I read that some financial experts had calculated the cost of working as $9 to $25 per hour. I was stunned! This meant that many of us who worked were actually paying for the privilege of working.

I was inspired by the challenge of reducing our budget instead of increasing our salary. I have not filled this book with ideas on how to make money at home. Many other books have done a fine job of that. I've listed a few of these books in "Additional Resources," appendix C, for those interested in pursuing this option.

Many books have been written on how to be thrifty. Some are theoretical in their approach, filled with interviews with other frugal people and impersonal statistics. Some are focused on a specific way to save, such as reducing credit card debt or using grocery coupons. Others try to be broad but are too extreme, cutting back in every aspect of life whether it is cost effective or not.

There is nothing theoretical in this book. It is a testimony of our journey. We were a two-income yuppie family that chose to make a lifestyle change. We have lived out all of the advice I suggest here.

I look at saving money as a means to an end. It is a job I perform in order to afford my staying at home. I don't do the things that I share in this book just for fun. I enjoy my luxuries if and when I can afford them. Some people take pleasure in being frugal as a hobby. I, however, must be convinced of the savings return before I do something frugal. For example, I find little profit in reusing envelopes or dryer lint. Those activities may save a penny or two, but that would not be a good use of my time. If you only have a little time to invest in saving, it might as well be put to use in the most effective places.

I believe in putting your efforts to work where they will save you the most. That is why the book is organized as it is—from the greatest savings opportunity to the least. Groceries are the first and largest topic that I discuss, because it is where families can save the most. We were able to save $250 per month in this category alone. I discuss other topics where we also achieved significant savings. When added together with the elimination of working expenses (the cost of working), we made a large dent in what we spent—the savings adding up to what some people might earn at a job.

Some people already have thought of the ideas in this book, especially those with parents or grandparents who lived through the Depression. Those people knew how to make what was necessary and live without the unnecessary. Their wisdom has been lost, and many think we shouldn't have to live without the things we desire. But others have asked for help with creative ideas to cut costs in their lives. It is for these people that I wrote this book. My desire is to get their creative juices in motion so they can start thinking of ways to save and meet their goals.

Your spouse doesn't have to earn a high wage in order for you to live on one income. I know several families (including my own) who have willingly lived on less than half of what the average family in their area earns.

We have added another member to our family. We have pets. We go on vacations. We even buy nice things for our kids and for ourselves.

These principles really can make a difference.

What do you have to lose?

If I Can Do It, You Can Do It

*Y*ou might think that it comes naturally for me to be organized, self-disciplined, and to spend extra time shopping and baking. This isn't true. It doesn't come naturally for me. I share my background not out of vanity but to show you that anyone can learn to live frugally.

The first thing you should know is that I am not "tight." It is not in my nature. I do what I have to in order to reach a goal. I can (and do) return to my luxuries in a snap when I can afford them. Some people are frugal because they have never known any other way. Others enjoy being frugal even though they can afford not to be. I knew what the "good life" was, but I was able to learn to live frugally when it was necessary to do so.

Until the age of eight, I lived in a Northern California suburb, Walnut Creek. My family lived an average middle-class life with a three-bedroom house, a dog, and simple vacations to Yosemite and the beach. Then life changed radically. My dad accepted a job with an American organization in Pakistan and then later moved to Nigeria. When the plane landed overseas, our life was never the same. We suddenly had five servants and a three-story house with bedrooms the size of most living rooms. All of our chores were done for us. I never had to clean my room or make my bed (I still don't make my bed). We even had coffee (or cocoa) brought to our rooms to awaken us in the morning. We traveled around the world several times in the six years that we lived overseas. We returned to the United States when I was fifteen, buying a three-bedroom house in Silicon Valley (south of San Francisco).

I share this to help you understand that I knew what good things were, but I have been able to learn to do without them. I was used to the convenience of having meals made and work done for me by others, so learning to apply myself to the art of being thrifty was new to me. The skills that I have acquired and share in this book were necessary to reach my financial goal of staying at home with my kids. It didn't all come to me at once. I started with one idea, then added another one later once the first one became second nature. Eventually I started to see a difference. Even if you only apply one or two ideas from this book, you will help your budget.

So if I can do it, you can do it!

Coming Home Stories
WHAT SOME MOMS SAY ABOUT THEIR DECISION

$ \quad $ \quad $

Taking the plunge and quitting your job is a scary step. It's riddled with consequences and fears about those consequences. Will we have enough money? Am I doing the right thing?

Most women I talk to are glad they quit. Many reveal their fears were unfounded, and that things were not as hard as they expected. Almost all report seeing benefits in their children and in themselves since being at home.

Coming home can bring a calm back to the family, a peaceful stability rather than a rushed schedule. A parent the kids can rely on to be there when they need her. There is nothing more devastating to a child than being told that he can't come home even though he doesn't feel well because Mom doesn't have any more time off. The rewards of a job are fleeting compared to the rewards of raising and shaping a future adult. But I don't want you to take only my word for it.

I get letters weekly from women who share their stories of the transition from working mom to at-home mom or mostly-at-home mom. They are heartening to anyone fearing the changes coming home might bring. Following are a few excerpts from these letters to encourage you. For more of these stories, please visit my Web site at *www.miserlymoms.com*.

19

For more on the subject of coming home, please read the books listed at the end of this chapter.

Shelly of Virginia

Deciding to quit work to be at home with my children at the age of thirty-five was no easy decision. I had worked all my adult life. It's been over a year since I came home to be with my children, and I wouldn't trade it for the world. I had always said that I could never stay at home with the kids, that I was a working kind of girl and that's the way it was. God in my life changed all that and so did my three great kids. I do day care in my home, trying to help other moms who think they have to work as well. I am always encouraging them to cut costs so they can come home to be with their own kids as I have. The extra money pays the groceries and another bill or two, so it's a financial help to say the least.

I strongly encourage any women who have the least bit of desire to quit work and come home—to look at every avenue, because, trust me, all the money in the world can't buy your happiness. One expense I cut without realizing it was medical costs. It's amazing how when you don't have that kind of stress in your life, and your kids aren't exposed to everyone else's sicknesses, you don't have to visit the doctor so often and spend your money there and at the drugstore. That's a big savings in itself. Where there's a will there's a way, and believe me, it's worth it in the long run. You'll never regret it!

Kate of Pennsylvania

At first my husband didn't get it. He anticipated dual incomes and all the things that could be done with that money. I have had to work on his thinking a lot to get him to see that there is no bigger payoff than a happy home and happy children. I never have to worry about coordinating schedules or who will watch my kids if they get sick. We aren't rich financially, but we are spiritually.

$\mathcal{D}$ONNA OF NEW YORK

When my husband and I were first married, we had quite a bit of debt. We were paying off our debt and thinking we were on the right track. Then things changed. We had our first baby, and I left my stressful job to work part time in a grant-funded position.

And then we bought a house.

And then we got pregnant again.

And then our car died.

And then the roof caved in.

And then my grant-funded position was cut.

And then I started to cry.

After the crying, getting hit unexpectedly with other hard and heavy bills, and being in lots more debt, I started to wise up. This reality check made me realize how unfrugal I was. My dear husband, who loved to spend money (before we were married he ate out every night and didn't even know you could pay more than a minimum monthly payment on a bill!), was very supportive in my endeavor. I started reading the experts (*Miserly Moms* and *Tightwad Gazette*, among others) and got into a positive frame of mind—that this was the best thing to do. Once I felt proactive and money-smart rather than desperate and "cheap," I realized my life had changed for the better. I started cooking almost everything from scratch, grocery shopping at different stores, mending clothes, shopping at Salvation Army, and finding lots of free family stuff to do.

Now we are down to one last debt, and it's steadily going down—any extra money we get goes toward it. We still love to go away, but now our trips involve driving and staying with family or at hostels, and finding free stuff to do while bringing our food along. My wonderful husband and I are so proud of what we are doing to make our lives better. We are not materialistically wealthy—our wealth and riches are much, much greater than that.

$\mathcal{C}$INDY OF NORTH CAROLINA

My husband and I have been married for fourteen years and have three children. For most of that time, I was working full time as a newspaper copy editor. Because we worked opposite shifts, day care wasn't an issue—but we didn't see much of each other! When my third child was a year old, we decided I could come home. Two months after coming home, that son was diagnosed with spinal muscular atrophy, which meant wheelchairs, ramps, ventilators, physical therapy, doctors, more doctors . . . and the list goes on. Though our insurance was good, it wasn't *that* good. So back to work I went.

Three years and piles of medical bills later, another son was diagnosed with Tourette's syndrome and learning disabilities. More bills. More stress. Lots more tears. Our marriage was rocky, I was unhappy, my husband was unhappy, the kids were unhappy. Nothing was getting done well. We decided to try coming home again. This time I prepared. We cashed in investments to pay off a car loan and other debts and cancelled the "extras"—cable TV, cell phone, etc. I switched from the convenient, swanky grocery store to the one with no perks and immediately saved $25 a week. We stopped going out to eat every Sunday after church, saving more than $100 a month. I stopped going to the bagel shop every morning, saving $10 a week. Funny thing is, after cutting out the little things, we had just as much at the end of the paycheck as we had when we were both working!

It's been nine months since I left my job, and I doubt I'll ever go back. The amount of stress that walked out the door when I came home has been astounding. I'm not always hurrying the kids because I have to get ready for work. My husband isn't stressed about hurrying home so I can go to work. We don't have to worry about sudden changes in one of the schedules. The kids are more relaxed. We're more relaxed.

Money is still tight, and because of our children's medical needs, it probably always will be. Even the children understand the benefits. I often hear them say how glad they are that they get to come home after school and don't have to go to day care. Many of my daughter's friends come home to an empty house. They are all glad that they get to enjoy a real summer vacation— no rushing to day care or day camps, etc. And they all understand that the cost of their *not* going to day care is fewer material things. Their cousin has all the latest toys and lives in a huge house—but she is not home to enjoy them. My kids actually *get it*!!! It's been a long journey home, but worth every minute!

ELLEN OF OKLAHOMA

I was a successful paralegal with a promising career in a fantastic firm. My husband and I both worked long, hard hours and had a nice home, two cars, and plenty of extras. Then I got pregnant. I wanted to stay at home, as my mother had, but we just couldn't make the math work out. We had decided that I would try working full time, but part of the time in the office and part of the time at home with a computer commute option.

Then five days after our daughter was born, my husband looked at me and said, "Whatever it takes, you're not going back to work." How I had prayed for his cooperation in this effort.

We slashed our budget. Took out all the extras. Stopped eating out, no car phone, no impulse shopping. I shop nice quality resale stores for clothes for all of us. It's amazing what you can do when you get creative and determined to make it all work out! Our food bill is a constant challenge to me to find new and cheaper options. *Miserly Moms* has recently given me new incentive to get devoted to budget cutting again. And I am so glad I'm the one raising my daughter—not an endless rotation of day-care workers. In the beginning we were afraid to even try. Now with an eighteen-month-old daughter, we can't imagine living any other way.

ANNE OF PENNSYLVANIA

I fully expected that the first six months would be painful and that I'd feel some regret about our decision. It's been six months now, and what I find instead is that this was the best decision for our family, and we are all reaping the rewards. Life is sane again, our kids are happy, the finances are manageable, and my stress level is low. Do I miss work? Nope. After years of high-level stress, it is the greatest relief to let all of that go. I have the mental energy to manage our home, finances, and lifestyle, which is challenge enough! I am happy with the lifestyle we now have, and despite several enticing opportunities to return to work, I remain steadfast in my commitment. It has all been worth the pain of self-examination and change. Do I recommend it for other families? You betcha!

ℒISA OF CALIFORNIA

Most people know that military pay is not elaborate, but my husband and I had always agreed about the importance of my being home with our children, for which I am most thankful. Prior to our marriage I had worked as a secretary/administrative assistant but knew in my heart that this was not something I wanted to continue once I was a mom. At the time we made less than $17,000. Yet I don't have any memories whatsoever of feeling bad about my decision. Through any financial challenge I truly believe that God blessed our choice. We always had enough food, our bills were paid, and I was able to be with my daughter.

The interesting thing about staying home is that many can manage it, but not many think they can. I truly believe there are just a few types of people who might not be able to—like single moms or widows. But I even know of some of these moms who are able to! I believe it all comes down to how willing/unwilling you are to slash expenses in your life and to take the time to make these changes.

These days I am a mom-at-home who also has health challenges. I still would not have it any other way. My job here is being the "home manager." I don't get paid for it, but I get great satisfaction knowing that I am making my husband's salary stretch as far as possible, and that we still are able to live as we originally intended. I see too many couple friends of ours struggling to work, get day care for their kids, commute, get supper on the table, and get everything else done they need to accomplish before the next day—only to start all over again! And do you know what? Most of them are not any better off than we are.

𝒯ERRI OF TEXAS

I was a marine biologist with several published papers and working for the government. I was shopping whenever I wanted to and buying just about whatever I wanted. My dear husband and I would go out to eat several times a week.

When I was pregnant, we had looked at several day cares we liked and picked one. But after the baby came, I knew I could not find it in my heart to go back to work. My husband said it would be okay for me to stay home as long as we could pay the bills. Now he wouldn't have it any other way, nor would I!

I am learning to cook, sew, raise animals, and enjoy the simple things in life! This has been the best decision I have made in my life as well as in the lives of my children. No one can take the place of a loving mother (or father) who stays home with the children. Material goods are nothing compared to the life and upbringing of a child. This time is so important to them. Don't cheat them out of time with you because of material things you "think" you need!

CHARLOTTE OF MASSACHUSETTS

We are a family of six, and I haven't worked since 1992. I am proud of myself, and my husband, for achieving this. I miss the indulgences of having extra money on hand, but when I stop to think about the blessings we possess, I am *so* grateful.

When one is surrounded by a wealthy (and therefore luxuriating) community, it is easy to become whiney, which saps the strength and the joy out of life.

KELLY OF OREGON

Having been on both sides of the fence, I wholeheartedly agree that there are actually very few families that absolutely need to have both parents working; and where at all possible one parent should be at home for the kids. More and more families are making this decision, and I would not be surprised to see more one-income families than two-income families in the near future.

TRACY OF ARIZONA

I spent all of my twenties working in offices, taking classes, and trying to make a career. I thought true satisfaction came through being successful in business (back in my Femi-Nazi days). But for all my hard work, I realized after twelve years of devoting my life to a "career" that I had gotten nowhere great. I was making decent money but nothing spectacular. What I noticed mostly was that I was really dissatisfied being a slave to a company.

Coming home has been one of the most important steps I've taken in my life. I now have a baby daughter, and I can't even imagine putting her in day care or with a baby-sitter all day. To me, being home and being a mother is the best job I've ever had!

RESOURCES

At-Home Motherhood: Making It Work for You, Cindy Tolliver (Resource Publication, 1994).

Coming Home to Raise Your Children: A Survival Guide for Moms, Christine Field (Revell, 1995).

Home by Choice, Brenda Hunter (Multnomah Books, 2000).

So You Want to Be a Stay-at-Home Mom, Cheryl Gochnauer (InterVarsity Press, 1999).

The Stay-at-Home Mom: For Women at Home and Those Who Want to Be, Donna Otto (Harvest House Publishers, 1997).

Staying Home Instead: How to Balance Your Family Life, Christine Davidson (Jossey-Bass, 1998).

Staying Home: From Full-Time Professional to Full-Time Parent, Darcie Sanders and Martha Bullen (Spencer & Waters, 1999).

Women Leaving the Workplace, Larry Burkett (Moody Press, 1999).

The Eleven Miserly Guidelines

$ $ $

*T*he art of being miserly interested me when I needed to find a creative alternative to working. When I quit my job, we had planned to move to a less expensive area. Then shortly after deciding not to move, I became pregnant again. Having already decided to stay home with our first child instead of returning to work, that door was now firmly shut (who's going to hire a pregnant woman?). Since I was not going to bring in money by working, I decided to attack the problem from the other side—by reducing the amount of money that went out of the house.

The first thing I did was to identify those items in our budget that were not fixed. That included any expense that fluctuated (such as food, gasoline, clothes, utilities). My next plan was to chip away at these expenses. I started with the highest bill—groceries. The Eleven Miserly Guidelines were originally notes that I kept in a binder for myself for reducing my grocery bill—the highest expense after our mortgage. I never intended to share the guidelines with anyone. But friends kept on borrowing my notes, wanting to learn how to save money. With the encouragement of friends, I wrote some articles, then the first edition of *Miserly Moms*. As I learned more and expanded my horizons beyond the grocery store, I added more notes to my notebook. Even though the Eleven Miserly Guidelines pertain mainly to food, the general principles can be applied to other areas of your household.

By doing some rethinking on how I shopped and cooked, I immediately lowered our food bill from $100 per week to $65 per week. That was a savings of $140 the first month. As I learned more ways to save and applied them, I spent less money. These ways to save eventually became my eleven guidelines. I was able to lower our food bill to $40 per week on many occasions. This, of course, can only happen if all eleven guidelines are being applied faithfully. We averaged between $60 to $65 per week on groceries, mainly because I bought few convenience items. Ten years later, and now a family of four, our food bill averages $85 per week. If we work hard at it, we can occasionally get it down to $65. A good goal to work toward is $15 per person per week. This total includes household needs such as paper towels, toilet paper, shampoo, etc.

If I compare this savings to the value of a part-time job, my budget cuts have proved to be more profitable. An average twenty-hour per week job (less taxes, baby-sitting, and other expenses) would provide only $1 per hour profit. I "earned" more than that applying my guidelines. If you believe that these ideas may be too much work for you, divide what you have saved on groceries in a week by the hours spent doing the shopping and cooking. It should reveal a decent savings—tax-free and at a minimal cost (the cost of gas used to drive to additional stores amounts to only $3 to $4 per week).

I have found many helpful resources to reduce our budget shortage. The most helpful have been cookbooks that contain recipes on how to make things yourself—cereals, jams, etc. The ones written in the late 1800s to the 1930s are my favorites. They are full of recipes for homemade versions of things that we think can only be purchased ready-made. Some of my favorites are listed at the end of chapter 8, "Make Your Own Whenever Possible."

With ideas gleaned from these "classics," I have formed some guidelines for grocery buying that make significant savings possible. In the following chapters, I have outlined the general guidelines along with some specific suggestions.

Some of these ideas may seem far-fetched; take what you like and leave the rest. For those just starting out on the odyssey of reduced spending, all eleven ideas may be overwhelming. After I spoke at a seminar, a woman came up to me "in distress." She thought she had to apply all eleven ideas immediately. As I told her, take one step at a time. Pick one idea and apply it. When it becomes comfortable, apply another one. Even if you only choose to try a few of the ideas, you will save. The more ideas you follow, the greater the savings.

THE ELEVEN MISERLY GUIDELINES

$ $ $

1. Don't confuse frugality with depriving yourself.
2. Remove little wasters of your money.
3. Keep track of food prices.
4. Don't buy everything at the same store.
5. Buy in bulk whenever possible.
6. Make your own whenever possible.
7. Eliminate convenience foods.
8. Cut back on meats.
9. Waste nothing.
10. Institute a soup and bread night (or baked potato night).
11. Cook several meals at once and freeze them.

$ $ $

CHAPTER THREE

GUIDELINE 1:

Don't Confuse Frugality With Depriving Yourself

$ $ $

*T*his is the most important aspect of being successful at saving money. If I think I am being cheap when I try to save money, I will never stick to my guidelines. My underlying goal of staying at home is more important than any guideline I try to follow. It is essential to my success.

When I first started my frugal lifestyle, I feared what it would involve. I believed that frugal people lived undesirable lives: wearing stained and torn clothing or reusing plastic wrap. I refused to participate in any of that. But such a definition of a frugal lifestyle does not have to be yours. There are many degrees of frugal lifestyles. I was determined to maintain a sense of class and still be frugal.

If any money-saving activity makes you feel cheap or tight, you will eventually abandon your efforts. That is not the price we need to pay to reach our goals. I don't need to feel tight and cheap in order to stay home with my kids. There are ways to save money and keep my dignity. Unfortunately, many people think the two cannot be linked.

GOAL SETTING

As I have stated, I am not tight by nature. And I believe that one can maintain a sense of class while being frugal. I know many people who love to be thrifty, but not because they need to be. Rather, it is a hobby or an obsession with them. Many frugal newsletters advocate dumpster diving and reusing envelopes and dryer lint. I always have to ask myself, "Why?" Are these things really worth the time? What do they pay you in terms of reaching your goals? A reused envelope saves you a penny. Dumpster diving may turn up things you can use, but did you need those things? Even if you did, what toxic elements were you exposed to in order to save a few dollars?

While I was working, many women I knew wanted to be at home with their kids, but most believed the price of staying home would be too high. These were career women who were used to good clothes, nice vacations, eating out regularly, and extra cash for impulse buying. They believed that in order to live without their income, they would have to resort to a cheap and undesirable lifestyle. So most remained working. I am living proof that there is a balance between these two.

In order to make any of the ideas in this book work for you, you must be very clear about why you are making the changes. Keep your goal at the forefront of your mind. Write it down and put it in an obvious place if you need the reminder. Next to the written goal, put a picture of something that helps to remind you of that goal. Without a clear goal or reason for change, you will abandon it quickly.

All of the following guidelines are tools for reaching the goal you have written down. Some will be harder to follow than others. Some may sound extreme. Just remember that all of the changes you make are for a good reason—reaching your ultimate goal. You might need to start thinking about your desires in terms of "needs" and "wants." Some things you think are necessary may actually be "wants" and could be exchanged for more money toward real needs. Some things you spend money on may have to wait. Our society tells us that we should have what we want *now*. That's not reality. We need to revisit the thinking of our elders who knew the virtue of saving up for things and doing without until they could afford them.

When I grumble about cutting corners, I remind myself of my goal. Mine is to stay home with my kids. Yours might be a vacation or buying a home. I look at eating leftovers and eating out less often as ways to reach my financial goals instead of something that I have to do. We still go on vacations, but less extravagant ones. We still eat out, but less often. I remind myself that the temporary luxury of a prepackaged meal, a shopping spree, or a meal out is less important than reaching my goal. And it doesn't take very much time.

Money and class are not synonymous. We can be classy and thrifty at the same time. I'm not saying that it's always easy. I enjoy nice things and going somewhere on impulse. Always planning for everything is hard. That's why we need to have a written reminder of our goal and some incentive boosters to help when we feel uninspired. Here are two of my favorites:

- *Track your success.* Divide the savings of one week by the hours spent saving it (shopping, cooking). Calculate the amount "earned" per hour. For example, last week I saved $60, and it took me seven hours to do it. That means I made $8.50 profit per hour—tax-free, no sitters, negligible expenses.
- *Have a visual reminder.* Put the budgeted grocery money in an envelope. You can see the leftover money when the week is over. That's yours to spend however you wish.

Hanging on to your reasons for being frugal will make the rest of the guidelines easier to hang on to as well. If you find your new frugal changes difficult to adjust to, remember that it's not our circumstances that define our life but how we view our circumstances.

CHAPTER FOUR

GUIDELINE 2:

Remove Little Wasters of Your Money

$ $ $

*W*hen I kept track of everything I spent over a month's time, I was surprised at how many times I had squandered money. Going over receipts is an activity that I recommend to anyone who is serious about saving money.

Those little trips to Target and lunches out at McDonald's will keep you from reaching your financial goals. It is amazing how much of a drain they are on the budget. When I feel like dropping into The Golden Arches or going to Target, I remind myself that those trips make things unattainable that are a higher priority on my list. Those trivial buys here and there can wipe out all that you have saved. One lunch per week at a fast-food restaurant costs $16 per month per person. That's close to $50 per month if my kids and I eat lunch out once per week. I could apply that toward a bill or vacation fund.

I have friends who "need" to shop for recreation and who work full time to pay for it. I wonder if the recreation is to ease the stress of work or the work is to pay for the recreation. In either case, the drains need to be plugged if any progress is to be made in reaching financial goals.

We must reprogram our thinking about money. It should

never be used to make ourselves feel good or to be a measure of someone's love for us. Money should be looked at as a tool. It's there to get you where you need to go. And if you don't have a plan for it, it will be wasted. A budget is a plan for our money much like a date book is a plan for our time.

$\mathcal{B}$UDGETING

In order to meet my goals, I have to make a budget and I stick to it. Anything I want to do that isn't budgeted has to wait until I save enough for it. The importance of a budget cannot be understated. It is your tool to making everything work.

The first step in budgeting is to see where your money is going. Make a list of all the expenses you have every month. If you have a computer, get a software program that will keep track of your expenses as it reconciles your checkbook. (We use a program called *Quicken* by Intuit for this purpose.) As you enter each check, the program asks for an expense category (no fair getting cash for everything). You can then run reports to see how much was spent in each category. This is very enlightening. *Quicken* is not the only program that offers these features. Among others, there is Microsoft's *Money*, Kiplinger's *Simply Money*, and Larry Burkett's *Money Matters*. None of these programs is a ready-made budget, nor is buying one necessary to construct a budget or to track expenses. You can do it manually with paper and pencil. Either way, keeping track of expenses will save you a lot of time and effort in maintaining your family budget.

The second step is to list your usual sources and amount of income for each month. If you have a fluctuating income, such as commissions, take an average over the past six months, or budget using the base amount/lowest amount as the source for bare essentials (rent, food, utilities), and use the extra commissions for everything else. If the extra commissions exceed your needs that month, put the extra aside for the lean months.

Once you have an idea of your expenses and income, then you can plan. The first thing you must do is to see if the income matches the expenses. If the expenses are greater, then some limits need to be put on your spending. Of course, there are some expenses you cannot reduce because they are fixed. This book focuses on the adjustable expenses, with groceries being the most variable. I found money for the fixed expenses by taking it out of the adjustable expenses. Other changes may need to be made, such as selling a car with a high monthly payment and buying a less expensive or used car instead.

To know if you are even close to a healthy budget, consult the experts. Larry Burkett has made recommendations for household budgets in his 1993 pamphlet *A Guide to Family Budgeting*. His suggestions may not match the cost of living for your area, but they are a place to begin. I personally find the first category too low with many families spending as much as 50 percent of their budget on housing. If this is your case, giving something up in another category may be necessary. Here are his suggestions:

LARRY BURKETT'S SUGGESTED BUDGET
(after taxes and tithe)

- 38% Housing (rent/mortgage, utilities, phone, household needs)
- 12% Food
- 15% Cars (maintenance, payments)
- 5% Debts
- 5% Insurance (life and homeowner's)
- 5% Medical/Dental (bills and insurance)
- 5% Entertainment (includes cable TV)
- 5% Clothing
- 5% Savings
- 5% Miscellaneous

This is just a sample of the many learning tips available for budgeting. I have done a more exhaustive discussion of the topic in my book *Frugal Families—Making the Most of Your Hard-Earned Money*. Instead of repeating the information here, I recommend you consult the book for more details.

GET ORGANIZED

Now that you have a plan (or budget) for your money, you need to know what bills need to be paid and when. Entering it all into a computer program is great, but if you don't know where the bills are or you forget to pay them on time, you will spend precious cash on late fees.

Put all your bills in one place. Every time the mail arrives, sort it. You don't have to open each envelope to do this. Just put all the bills in one location—immediately as they arrive. By doing this, you reduce the risk of misplacing a bill and forgetting about it.

On every month of your calendar or date book, write down when you need to pay your bills. Most of my bills are due in the first ten days of the month, so on the thirtieth of every month, I write, "Pay bills." This way I don't forget to pay them and I avoid late fees.

Have a checklist of bills that are to be paid every month. As you pay each bill, check it off on your list. Make sure all bills have arrived. Sometimes a bill gets lost in the mail. This is no excuse for not paying it—you're still responsible for it and will be charged late fees if it doesn't get paid. If a bill hasn't arrived by bill-paying day, call the company and get the amount due and mailing address for the payment. Their phone number is on the previous month's statement. The customer's section of the bills that have been paid should be stored in a box or folder for record-keeping purposes. Don't throw them away.

You also need to keep track of how you are doing with your spending throughout the month. Some people balance their checkbook several times a month. Others review their budget and spending every few weeks. I keep an index card in my checkbook that has eight columns—one for each major budget category that I might use while away from the house. At the top of each column I write the amount budgeted in that category. Every time I write a check, I record the amount in the appropriate column. Once the numbers in that column add up to what is budgeted for the month, I can't spend any more in that category. If I borrow from another column, I must be sure I can do without that amount for that category for the rest of the month.

By keeping track in this way, there are no surprises at the end of the month, like bounced check fees. We cannot "hope" that we will stay within our budget. We must actively make it happen.

DEBT REDUCTION

Debt is usually one of the main obstacles to balancing a budget. The car payment, the mortgage payment, and the credit card payments take a good share of the average household income. Once these are under control, life becomes less stressful. Most people have several credit cards (Visa or MasterCard), a department store card, and gas cards. In the U.S., the average household credit card balance is $3,900. And one in seven card holders says they are "in over their heads."

The first step is to learn to live within the boundaries of our income. Stop using credit cards for anything other than a true emergency. (Eating out and buying new clothes are not emergencies.)

Don't rush out and cut up your cards. Sometimes they are necessary (for renting a car or making hotel reservations). Instead, keep one or two cards and control your spending. If you are using credit cards regularly and not paying them off in full each month, then you are outside of your budget. Put the cards away in a safe place. Don't carry them with you (unless you travel). Regard them as emergency tools only. Most situations allow you to go home and get the card and come back.

Second, start rethinking the debts that you have. Do you have a car payment that is more than you can afford? Maybe you need a less expensive car. Can you refinance for a lesser rate?

Third, make a plan to repay your debts. You must get rid of the debt as quickly as possible. If it takes a few years, don't despair. It's those small yet faithful steps that will get you to your goal of financial freedom. Several organizations offer tools and free help in assessing your debts and making a plan to deal with them. One plan I like is on the Internet: "The Debt Reduction Planner" offered by *Quicken*. "The Debt Reduction Planner" will ask you for information about your debts and help you build a plan to get out of debt. You'll have a chance to compare your current situation against your new plan and make adjustments. And you'll get an action plan and links to other resources. Visit them at *www.quicken.com/saving/debt*.

Fourth, get rid of any high-interest-rate cards. Keep only one multipurpose credit card and make it one with no annual fee. For a list of credit cards with the lowest fees and interest rates, send $5 to CardTrak, P.O. Box 1700, Frederick, MD 21702, call (800) 344–7714, or visit their Web site at *www.cardtrack.com*.

Fifth, consolidate your bills to the lowest interest rate available. This may be the one credit card you have, or it may be a loan from your credit union or savings and loan. Some people consolidate their loans and then refinance their homes so that their overall monthly payments are lower. This is okay if you already were going to refinance the home due to lower interest rates. Nevertheless, beware: sometimes this new lower total payment is deceptive. Even though the combined payments are lower, the overall balance of debt may now be higher, since you added the high expense of refinancing (points, fees, etc.) and you have just reset the clock on your mortgage back thirty years. I know of families who are unable to retire, realizing the mortgage they kept refinancing is too high to pay on a pension.

Sixth, faithfully pay as much as you can each month—or more. If a little extra cash comes your way, use it toward the debt. Every little bit helps.

Finally, if you are "in over your head," turn to a professional for help. There are credit counseling agencies everywhere. For a referral to a nonprofit credit counselor near you, call the National Foundation for Consumer Credit at (800) 388–2227, *www.nfcc.org*, the Consumer Credit Counseling Service (CCCS) at (800) 388-CCCS, or Christian Credit Counselors, Inc. at (800) 796-8709, *www.ibudget.org*. You can also look in the Yellow Pages under "credit counseling" for more local listings.

As with budgeting, I devote much more space to the topic of debt in my book *Frugal Families*, explaining in detail how to get out of debt. Not wanting to repeat myself, please consult that book for more information. I include lists of agencies to help you out and step-by-step ideas for getting out of debt. You may also want to review the resources listed at the end of this chapter.

MAKING IT WORK

For those who cannot control their spending, I suggest you leave your checkbook and credit cards at home. (Remember that most emergencies allow you to go home first.) Put the budgeted money into envelopes if you have to. Have a separate envelope for each category in the budget. Take the money out of the bank and keep it in the envelopes. When the envelope is empty, you will have to wait until the next scheduled bank trip. If keeping lots of cash around is a worry to you, only take cash out of the bank weekly. And only take cash for expenses you will be currently dealing with (groceries, household, gas).

Larry Burkett and other financial experts have marketed items to help you with a cash system. But you can do it cheaply. Use small envelopes and label the top right-hand corners so it's easy to see the categories when flipping through the envelopes. Or purchase an inexpensive plastic coupon file that will fit in your purse and label the sections.

If you have some self-control, keep your checkbook with you, but keep a running total of your spending throughout the month. As I said earlier, if we wait until the end of the month to see how we did on our spending, we usually will have overspent.

When we lost half our income, it was a matter of survival for the first year. I had to stick to a tight budget to keep from going under. I did whatever was necessary to remain frugal. If I had weak knees when I was near a department store or at the sight of a "sale" sign, I would turn my head. If impulse shopping at the grocery store overcame me, I shopped only once a month to avoid those temptations. The malls were too tempting for me, so I avoided them altogether. When I shared these ideas with people, some look shocked or said, "Oh, that's just too drastic." Nothing is too drastic if your goals are important enough to you.

RESOURCES

There are additional suggested books on budgeting and getting out of debt listed in appendix C.

Debt-Free Living: How to Get Out of Debt and Stay Out, Larry Burkett (Moody Press, 2000).

Dollars and Sense: Making the Most of What You Have, Wilson J. Humber (NavPress, 1993).

Down-Size Your Debt, Andrew Feinberg (Penguin Books, 1998).

How to Get Out of Debt, Stay Out of Debt, and Live Prosperously, Jerrold Mundis (Bantam Books, 1990).

Life After Debt: How to Repair Your Credit and Get Out of Debt Once and for All, Bob Hammond (Career Press, 1993).

Master Your Money, Ron Blue (Thomas Nelson Publishers, 1997).

Saving on a Shoestring: How to Cut Expenses, Reduce Debt, Stash More Cash, Barbara O'Neill (Dearborn Financial Publishing, Inc., 1995).

Two Incomes and Still Broke: It's Not How Much You Make, But How Much You Keep, Linda Kelley (Times Books, 1998).

Your Finances in Changing Times, Larry Burkett (Moody Press, 1993).

CHAPTER FIVE

GUIDELINE 3:

Keep Track of Food Prices

$ $ $

*W*hen I started my adventure of squeezing even more value from each dollar I spent, I thought I knew what most things cost. Someone suggested that I write prices down to see if I knew as much as I thought I did. This was the most educational activity I could ever do. Prices are *not* about the same everywhere.

I started to keep track of prices on foods in my local stores. At first I started writing down the regular retail price at each store for things I commonly used. Then I added the best sale price for those items at the same store. By adding the best sale price, I created a goal for myself. For every item I always included the size and unit price (cost per ounce or per pound) so I had an easy comparison. This is very important, as package sizes vary. Many companies are reducing the size of their containers instead of increasing their prices (e.g., tuna cans used to be 6½ ounces, but are now 6¼ ounces or less).

I keep this list in a small notebook (I use a pocket calendar) that easily fits in my purse. I created columns for food types and then rows for the brand name, price, and unit of measure information. Below is a sample of what's in my notebook.

COLD BOXED CEREAL

Store	Name Brand	Retail Price	Best Sale	Best Unit Cost
Store A	store brand "Cheerios"	$2.29	20 oz. @ $0.99	$0.05/oz.
Store B	Cheerios	$3.99	20 oz. @ $1.99	$0.10/oz.
Warehouse club	Cheerios	40 oz. @ $6.29		$0.16/oz.
Store A	Quaker Granola	16 oz. @ $3.69	16 oz. @ $2.39	$0.15/oz.
Homemade	granola	16 oz. @ $0.99		$0.06/oz.

By breaking items down to their unit price, I can see at a glance where an item is the least expensive. And surprisingly (to many), it isn't cheapest at the warehouse store.

From this list I began creating goals for myself. I try not to buy an item for more than the best sale price that I have seen. This becomes my target. If we don't have a target to aim for, we settle for what's available. For those of you just starting out, I have included a sample of some of my target prices. This is meant to help you get started in your shopping. These prices are an average of prices across the country. Your region may have higher or lower sale prices.

PRICE GOALS

Food Item	Once in a Blue Moon	A Good Sale	Average Price
Drink mix (makes 1 qt.)	$ .10	$ .25	$ .50
Ground meat:			
Beef (1 lb.)	.88	1.00	2.39
Turkey (1 lb.)	.50	.69	1.69
Chicken (parts, per lb.)	.29	.49	1.69
Chicken breast (per lb., boneless, skinless)	1.79	1.99	4.99
Tuna (per 6¼ oz. can)	.25	.50	.79
Dry cereal (14 oz.)	.99	1.69	3.99

Granola (per lb.)	.99	1.69	2.50
Butter (per lb.)	.99	1.50	2.29
Margarine (per lb.)	.33	.50	.89
Toilet paper (per roll)	.20	.25	.35
Paper towels (per roll)	.45	.50	.99
Apples (per lb.)	.49	.69	1.29
Potatoes (per lb.)	.10	.20	.30
Vegetable oil (per oz.)	.03	.04	.09
Cheese (per lb.)	1.59	2.99	3.99
Flour (5 lb.)	.69	.99	1.69
Sugar (5 lb.)	1.39	1.69	2.29
Spaghetti (1 lb.)	.39	.69	.79
Cake mix	.79	.99	1.29
Mac & cheese (generic)	.20	.25	.89
Frozen juice concen.	.69	.99	1.29
Salad dressing (per oz.)	.07	.08	.12
Turkey lunchmeat (per lb.)	2.50	2.99	3.89
Lettuce (head)	.50	.79	1.29
Broccoli (head)	.99	1.39	1.50
Light bulbs (ea.)	.25	.31	.50
Laundry detergent (per oz.)	.03	.04	.06
Kleenex (175 ct.)	.89	.99	1.59

I set target prices for other items as well. I know at what price I can get something, and I avoid paying much more for it. For example, I know that a homemade dinner for four people usually costs me $3 to $4. This is easy to achieve. Having this goal keeps me from ordering a $20 pizza or spending $35 for dinner at a restaurant. You can do the same with other categories, such as clothing or toys. I have included some of my cost goals for meals to help you begin setting goals for yourself.

COST GOALS

SNACKS

Key to saving in this area: Buy only one snack item per week—when it's gone, they have to wait!

- Make homemade instead of store-bought (popcorn, popcorn balls, pumpkin bread, cinnamon toast, cookies)
- Eat fruit and veggies with dips (homemade)
- Visit day-old bread outlets for cookies, chips, and crackers

Price Goal: 5–10¢ per person/per snack

BREAKFAST

Key to saving in this area: Avoid (or reduce use of) dry cereals and prepackaged mixes.

- Make homemade alternatives (muffins, pancakes from scratch, French toast, eggs, hot cereal)

Price Goal: 25¢ per person/per meal

LUNCH

Key to saving in this area: Avoid convenient mixes and premade foods.

- Avoid fast food and other restaurants
- Make homemade sandwiches with lunchmeat on sale
- Make homemade soups
- Put homemade juice in a thermos—avoid juice boxes
- Use leftovers from other meals

Price Goal: 75¢ per person/per meal
Notes: Invest in a lunch-box-size freezer pack so the kids can take perishable items to school (tuna sandwich, lunchmeat, leftovers). Also invest in a small thermos for soup and one for juice.

DINNER

Key to saving in this area: Avoid convenient mixes and premade foods.

- Avoid fast food and other restaurants
- Stretch the meat with vegetables, grains, and beans

Price Goals: Budget meal for 4: $1 total
Average meal for 4: $3 total
Special meal (seafood, roast) for 4: $5+ total

CHAPTER SIX

GUIDELINE 4:

Don't Buy Everything at the Same Store

$ $ $

*O*f the eleven guidelines, I believe this one has been the greatest source of savings for me. Although planning for and shopping at several stores is the biggest time expenditure in the "job" of being miserly, it provides the biggest payoff. It can save you up to 50 percent of your grocery bill.

No one store has the lowest price on everything—not even the warehouse clubs. As I learn more about the art of being miserly, my bills keep dropping. There are two main stages to shopping: planning, and deciding where to buy. If you do these two stages while rolling through the grocery aisles, you won't save anything. You must become aware of who sells what, and what each item costs. You can incorporate coupons and rebates, but they must be secondary to where and what you decide to buy. Below is an explanation of how I do my planning and shopping.

*P*LANNING

The worst mistake shoppers make is to show up at the grocery store and simply buy whatever they think they'll need that week. Even if you choose to do all of your shopping in one store, just having a list will reduce your spending. Planning is essential to your saving success. Most people think of planning as picking their menus for the week, making a list, and buying those things at the nearest store. I want to challenge you to rethink your planning and shopping process.

Instead of making a random menu plan and shopping around it, plan the menu and lists around the grocery sales. One friend of mine saved $30 the first time she switched her planning style. She didn't apply any of the other tips in the book. She just planned the menu around the sale items instead of picking recipes randomly.

The best way to prepare for a shopping trip is to read the sale flyers from local grocery stores, which are often found in the food section of the newspaper. Build a menu plan around these sale items. The items on the front and back pages are called "loss leaders," because the store is losing money on those items. Don't forget to plan your produce needs around those listed on the front or back page of the flyer. I save even more if my menus are based on low-cost recipes found in my favorite frugal cookbooks. After I make my menus based on sale items, I make grocery lists for each store. And if the loss leader is not as low as your target price is for that item, use what you have stored from a previous bulk buy and skip that week's loss leaders.

COUPONS AND REBATES

Coupons can be helpful for saving money. We just need to use them wisely and not let the coupon direct us.

Some people are opposed to using coupons under any circumstances. Their reasons vary. The most common complaint is that coupons increase the price of food, because the manufacturer must recover the costs somewhere. This is a valid concern. But boycotting coupons will not drive the prices back down again. A good example of this was a marketing strategy of Proctor and Gamble. Many people wrote asking them to stop issuing coupons and lower their prices instead. As a test, they did stop issuing coupons, but they did not lower any prices. They reinstated the use of coupons after numerous complaints from consumers.

Many manufacturers won't drop coupons for that reason. Even

though only 3 percent of consumers use coupons, manufacturers continue to spend millions of dollars printing and distributing them. Coupons cost them less than reducing all their prices. They believe that a coupon is a discount available for those who want to make the extra effort, and for maintaining good relations with those same (but few) consumers.

I have noticed that coupons are usually for convenience foods that I can make myself or do without. Rarely do you see a coupon for meat, bread, or milk. With a coupon, I am tempted to buy something that I normally would not buy—just because I have a coupon. When I am tempted to buy an item because I have a coupon, I ask myself three questions: (1) Do I need it? (2) Can I buy it cheaper in another brand? (3) Can I prepare it cheaper myself?

It's important to compare the price of the name-brand item with the coupon to the price of an off-brand item without a coupon. Even with a coupon, the name-brand item may still cost more than the off-brand item at its regular price. And the off-brand items are not inferior in most cases. Actually, many off-brand items are name-brand items bought at a discount (surplus) and then relabeled.

A good sale matched with a coupon can be a good deal. And it can be an even greater deal if a store offers double coupons and has a sale at the same time. Or the store may be having a buy-one-get-one-free sale and they offer double coupons. But be aware that most stores offering double or triple coupons have higher prices on most of their groceries. I usually purchase the items I have good coupons for and take the rest of my list somewhere else.

Take advantage of the coupon books mailed out by stores. These stores hope to draw you in with your entire week's grocery list. If you just buy the coupon items, you can save big. Remember to take the rest of your list to the cheapest store nearby. With these coupon books, I make a monthly trip to stock up on the cereals, soups, and other items. Each time I make this trip with the coupon book, I get $30-$40 taken off at the register.

You can maximize your savings if you use a manufacturer's coupon at the same time you use a store coupon. It is legal to do this, since one is issued by the store and the other by the food manufacturer. For example, the store selling Cheerios for $3.99 may also be having a buy-one-get-one-free sale. You have a $1.00-

off-two-boxes cash register coupon from your last visit and a manufacturer's coupon from the Sunday newspaper for $1.50 off two boxes. Using all three deals is legal and a real steal (two boxes for $1.49, or $0.75 each)!

Places to find good coupons are the Sunday newspapers, local library coupon exchange boxes, local coupon clubs, and even the Internet. If your library doesn't have an exchange box, ask if you can start one.

Visit Web sites that allow you to print your own grocery coupons, such as Smart Source (*www.smartsource.com*) and Cool Savings (*www.coolsavings.com*). Many coupon sites offer printable coupons, but not for grocery items. Avoid any Web sites that offer bank account credit instead of free coupons.

Another source of coupon savings are Web Bucks through *www.supermarkets.com*: they offer a customized list of discounts at your local supermarket. Start by entering your zip code and selecting the supermarket you want. The site will show you a listing of offers available at that store. Select the offers you want, then print the "ValuPage" and bring it to the store. At the checkout counter, give the cashier your printout to scan. At the end of your order, a coupon will be printed by the clerk with Web Bucks that can be used like cash on your next purchase.

Another good way to get coupons of high value is to write a note of appreciation (or complaint) to the manufacturer of a product you use. They usually send several valuable coupons for your trouble.

Once you have some coupons, keep them in a small portable filing system. I use a small expandable folder. I file by food category (snacks, breakfast, side dishes, vegetables, desserts, household items, baby items). Some people file alphabetically or by expiration date. Do whatever works best for you. However, the method won't do you any good unless you make sure the coupons are with you when you shop. One friend of mine gathers the coupons she'll need for that shopping trip and staples them to the shopping list so they won't be forgotten at home. I have given my list and coupons to my husband and seen him forget them at checkout time, so I staple the coupons to the check in the checkbook so there is no way he can forget.

Rebates can also be good, especially if matched with a sale and coupons. You may have heard stories of people spending only $20 for $120 worth of groceries by combining coupons, sales, and rebates. It can be done, but this is a rare event. And it isn't much of a savings if you have to buy things that you normally wouldn't buy just to get a rebate. There are avid rebate fans who spend up to twenty hours per week reading rebate newsletters, clipping, mailing, and filing grocery receipts and proof-of-purchase seals. I can't help but repeat myself—would I buy these things anyway? It would be cheaper (and take less time) to shop sales and cook more meals from scratch.

Overall, I do not encourage an excessive emphasis on coupons or rebates. There are coupon clubs and subscriber services for coupons/rebates. I think you eventually lose with these. The real savings is following the lowest price—whether that is a sale or an off-brand. Occasionally that lowest price may be the use of a coupon plus a sale. Then it is to your advantage. Remember that coupons and rebates are just among the many tools to help you get to your savings goal.

To illustrate this point, let me tell you about a shopping competition I participated in. I was invited to be a guest on *The Gayle King Show,* a TV talk show. I was there to compare my shopping style with another "grocery expert." The other expert was the creator of the Coup-O-Dex coupon filing system (a Rolodex made for coupons that rests on the grocery cart's handle). He believed in using coupons for everything he could. I was assigned a family to plan and shop for, as was he. We both shopped and met at the checkout counter (with cameras following our every move). When he checked out, he had $46 worth of coupons taken off his bill, leaving him with a final food bill of $72. When I checked out, I had no coupons, but my food bill was only $49. How? I had planned meals around the sale items and made things from scratch. He planned the meals around the coupons he had, which tend to be for the more expensive convenience items.

SHOPPING

Once my planning is done, I go to each store and buy only those items on my list. I first visit the more expensive stores and buy their good sale items on my list. Don't impulse buy. Don't look up and down the aisles for what's available. Again, it's important to remember that those stores with the greatest sale prices (or "loss leaders") and double or triple coupons tend to have higher prices on everything else. Their sale prices are great, but their other items tend to be 20 percent higher than most stores. They have to recover their losses somewhere. This is why it is important to buy only their sale items. I go to two or three stores this way, getting the sale items I need for my menus. I finish at the store that I find to be cheapest overall and buy their sale items and the rest of my grocery list.

Many people might say, "Why spend all that time going from store to store? A few cents saved at one store won't pay for the gas of hopping around." It's not just "a few cents" being saved, as you'll quickly realize after one week's worth of shopping. You might lose your savings if you drove long distances to the two or three stores that you choose. All the stores should be within ten miles of your home so gas isn't an issue. I figure that with each shopping trip I save $30 to $50 in groceries and only use $3 to $4 in gas.

I usually do all the shopping in one afternoon, as it is easier to finish all at once. Take a few days if it works better for you. Shop one store on the way home from somewhere. The short lists only take fifteen to twenty minutes. Or send your hubby to one of the stores with a precise list. Some weeks I find only two or three items on sale that interest me at the "secondary" stores. When this happens, I skip those stores that week. It has to pay off to go to the extra stores if you are going to do it.

Beware of the "great" sale! Sometimes a store announces a big-name item at a great price, but they only offer one of its products at that price. For example, a store recently advertised Oscar Mayer hot dogs at $1.50. The average store price is $2.49. But only one of Oscar Mayer's three types of hot dogs was offered at this price. The other two were over-priced at $3.99 each. Watch the fine print. There are certain stores that do this type of advertising regularly. If the store that you frequent is always out of the sale item, drop them from your shopping routine. Many stores purchase a limited stock of the sale item, hoping you will purchase a more expensive substitute. Ask for a rain check. Some stores won't give one until the last day of the sale. So shop there on the last day to get what's in stock and get the rest next week with the rain check.

To add even more savings, watch the flyers for free food items or super savings with purchases. Here you can save even more on your food bill. One week I got a ten-pound bag of potatoes and two cans of tuna—free. This converted into soup, a casserole, and potato salad. These are not the buy-one-get-one-free offers, but a coupon for a free item with a certain purchase. With either of these types of offers, don't buy things that you normally wouldn't buy just to get the free food. You don't gain anything that way.

TYPES OF STORES

You aren't alone in working to reach your goal. There are many types of stores to help the miserly mom. There are warehouse clubs, supermarkets, grocery outlets, specialty outlet stores, and more. They can make your job easier and hopefully help you stay on track. You must know how and when to use them. Let's look at each type of store.

Warehouse Clubs

The most well-known stores are the warehouse club stores, such as Costco or Sam's Club. These club stores can save you money, but only on certain things. I see people buying everything they need at these stores, thinking all their items are cheaper. You must know your prices before you shop there. Because this type of store is so popular, yet tricky to use, I have set aside an entire chapter to discuss their use ("Be Wary of Warehouse Clubs," chapter 16). The bottom line: shop sparingly at these stores.

Supermarket Warehouses

There are supermarket warehouses that offer bulk foods and minimal services (such as no baggers) to cut costs. Some of these might be Pak 'n' Save, Cub Foods, Rainbow Foods, and Food-4-Less. These stores carry a more limited variety of name brands than a regular grocery store does, but they do have good prices on their store-brand items. This is where I usually take the rest of my list. The only items that I have had trouble with are meats, fish, and milk (poor quality) and open bins of bulk foods (people put odd things in them). If you have small children, shopping at these can be stressful because you have to bag your own food, write your check, and care for the kids all at the same time.

Outlet Stores

There are also outlet stores that sell clothing, food, or specialty items at discount prices. These stores are usually listed by their company name (e.g., Oshkosh, Nike, Wonder, Hostess, Entenmann's, Oroweat, etc.). These are great places to find good bargains. The clothing outlets usually are not cheaper than a department store sale, but their clearance racks are great. The bread stores have half-price loaves of bread and other baked goods. Many have a "cheap" day when items are a dime apiece, and they offer frequent buyer's cards that allow you to earn free products.

Then there are general outlet stores that carry a variety of goods. Some of these examples may be in your area:

- *Trader Joe's,* which sells food items of their own brand as well as imported items.

   Good Buys: fish, breads, cereals, vitamins, dairy
- *Canned Food Grocery Outlet,* which sells surplus, outdated, discontinued, or dented items at good prices.

   Good Buys: all items
- *ALDI's,* which sells a variety of discounted food and goods.

   Good Buys: milk and diapers
- *Wal-Mart,* which sells a variety of goods and foods.

   Good Buys: most items

   Note: Many Wal-Mart stores will match grocery store flyer prices. The only drawback is that they don't carry many brands, so you have to negotiate a replacement brand with the clerk, who may ask you to wait for the manager. If you don't mind this hassle, it's worth it.
- *Cost Plus Imports,* which sells imported items, coffee, candy, and small toys very cheaply.

   Good Buys: gift items, coffee, candy
- *Dollar Stores,* which have good deals on food and household items. I have seen large salad dressings, liquid drain opener,

and cold medication all for ninety-nine cents each.

Good Buys: all items

- *PX/Military* have good overall prices. They are usually as cheap as you can get on sale at a regular grocery store. Use these if you have access to them.

Visit these stores and compare their prices to those you have written down from your local stores. They may be worth including in your shopping routine.

SHARE

SHARE is an organization that is not a store but is vital for thrifty shopping. It is a nonprofit worldwide co-op that allows its members to buy shares of food at greatly discounted prices. A share usually costs $8 to $15 depending on the food category. For example, a meat share is $8 and contains approximately six pounds of meat. A "regular" share costs $15 and contains approximately six to seven pounds of meat, several types of produce, some convenience foods, and some pasta or rice. There are also monthly specials you can buy. You can purchase as many shares per month as you wish. They order one day per month and deliver one day per month. It is an incredible savings on groceries.

SHARE is not a charity. A willingness to help oneself and to participate in helping others is at the foundation of all SHARE activities worldwide. The only membership fee they ask is that you volunteer two hours per month (per share that you purchase). So for one regular share and one meat share, you would be asked to volunteer four hours that month. You can volunteer anywhere in the community: your child's school, church, Little League, youth programs, playground duty, or at SHARE.

SHARE recently added the availability of coffee and a discount pharmacy to the list of benefits it brings to communities in the U.S. For a SHARE location near you, visit their Web site at *www.worldshare.org/join/Affiliates.html* or call them at (888) 742–7372.

CO-OPS

Another source for low-cost food is a co-op. They can provide organic (and other) products at a lower cost than most local

stores. Items that you might buy in a health food store are usually—but not always—much cheaper through a co-op. This is
where knowing your prices is essential.

Most co-ops are formed when some friends get together to buy
foods wholesale to save money. They find a wholesale co-op dis-
tributor that will allow new members in their area (many areas are
closed due to retail store pressure of the competition: retail stores
don't like wholesale outlets that sell the same manufacturers'
goods as they do). Someone does the ordering, receives the ship-
ment, divides the orders, and handles the money. Many groups
also hold meetings and seminars on nutritional cooking.

Many co-ops have gone to a mail-order style, where you get a
quarterly catalog and send in your request. These types of businesses usually sell in large quantities, such as a case of cereal boxes
or potato chips. This sort of buying is good for people who con-
sume a great deal of certain items, or who can split a case with
someone. Beware of the traps of being in a co-op. Some groups
require a minimum-dollar-amount purchase every month. This
can be binding if you don't need to buy or don't have the grocery
money for it that month. I have also found that I tend to overbuy
when I'm in a co-op. Even though something may be a great price,
I don't need twelve of them. I also tend to buy things at a co-op
that I normally wouldn't buy—just because it is wholesome and/
or a great deal. But do I really need it? Could I make it myself?

Check your phone book for cooperatives. Call a local university and ask them for a listing of co-ops in the area. Ask friends at
church or work—word of mouth is a great source of information.
If none of these provides help, visit the Cooperative Grocery online and see their directory of co-ops (*www.cooperativegrocer.com/
coopdir.html*). To order a printed copy of this directory, call them
at (800) 878–7333. You can also write to or call the National Cooperative Business Association, 1401 New York Ave. NW, Suite
1100, Washington, D.C. 20005, (202) 638–6222, or visit their Web
site at *www.cooperative.org*. They will give you the regional head-
quarters of cooperatives near you. If there isn't a co-op near you,
form one yourself.

Another great source of general information on all types of cooperatives is the Whole Co-op Catalog offered by Twin Pines Cooperative Foundation. They offer books and videos on how to start any

type of co-op (food, worker, housing, agricultural, baby-sitting). They also explain the legal and financial aspects of starting one and have directories of co-ops across the nation. You can call them at (916) 649–9757 or write to them at 216 F Street, PMP 1844, Davis, CA 95616, or visit their Web site at *www.dcn.davis.ca.us/go/actpcoop/* to receive a catalog.

EXCHANGING SERVICES

Many people are relearning the skill of exchanging services. I say "relearning," since this was the original form of business transaction in America. The early settlers bought and sold goods by offering something they had made in exchange—such as homemade cheese for a handmade woolen item. This form of business is still around. Many do it casually by finding something they can offer and asking someone if they would consider exchanging services with them. A friend of mine wanted to join a local pool for the summer but couldn't afford it. So she offered to paint their changing rooms in exchange for her family's membership. Other friends exchange lawn care, hair care, wedding services (cakes, flowers, music, photography), auto repair, ironing, sewing, etc.

For those with more elaborate needs or those who live where there are limited resources, there are national exchange or bartering groups. The groups list what you are interested in obtaining and offering. They usually charge a high annual fee for this service. I have found that many local churches offer such listings free of charge.

There are several bartering networks and clubs that you can join. Some are online groups that you can barter with anywhere in the U.S. These clubs work by charging a small transaction fee for posting services or goods for trade on the network. The service keeps track of the credits you have exchanged with another member. No money is exchanged, but the value of the goods or services is recorded. For example, if you were a writer and you wrote an article for a company's magazine, and you valued your work at $600, you have a $600 credit that you can use with any other member in the network. For a local bartering group, look in your Yellow Pages under "Barter."

Before joining a barter network, do some research. Your reputation, as well as trade credits, is at stake. Ask how large the network is, what categories for trade are available, how long the network has been operating (look for one that's been around at least five years), and what the members think about it (write to them and ask them). There is an agency that can run a background check on network exchanges for you: The International Reciprocal Trade Association. Send a self-addressed stamped envelope to IRTA, 6305 Hawaii Court, Alexandria, VA 22312.

Other places for doing research on the subject are on the Internet. Try visiting these sites:

www.i-barter.com	discussion groups for barterers
www.nate.org	The National Association of Trade Exchanges—a nonprofit organization that serves barter clubs and their members and can locate exchange networks near you
www.barternet.com	exchange network—offers exchanges worldwide
www.artofbarter.com	barter exchange network

I have never used a formal service for my exchange needs. I just arrange the exchange myself by asking an individual. As my mother always said, "You'll never know the answer until you ask."

ℒOCAL FARMS

Another source of savings are local farms and ranches. If you live near one, ask about discounts on eggs, milk, or poultry. Look for roadside stands near farms. Many homeowners who are avid gardeners set up a stand in their front yard to sell their extra produce. Write to the chamber of commerce for a list of any farms that allow you to pick your own produce.

If you live near a dairy, purchase milk and cheese there. If the trip is far, stock up. Both milk and cheese freeze fine. Eggs freeze well, but not in the shell. Crack them and freeze the insides in a plastic bag. I freeze two eggs per bag since most recipes call for two eggs. If you live near a chicken farm and can get a good deal on eggs, here are some tips on how to tell a good egg from a bad one:

To tell if an egg is fresh, place it in a pan of cold water.

- If the egg lies on its side, it is fresh.
- If it tilts, it is 3 to 4 days old.
- If it stands upright, it is probably 10 days old (use these for baking).
- If the egg floats to the top, it is very old and should not be used.

To add to my savings on eggs, I purchase two types of eggs. In California there was a local egg ranch that sold regular grade AA and "checks and dirties." The checks and dirties are eggs with imperfections in the shell. These eggs have a higher risk of contamination and shouldn't be eaten unless completely and thoroughly cooked, such as in baking. These imperfect eggs cost half the price of regular eggs.

RESOURCES

Personal and Business Bartering, James Harvey Stout (TAB Books, 1985).

Storefront Revolution: Food Co-Ops and the Counterculture, Craig Cox (University Press, 1994).

CHAPTER SEVEN

GUIDELINE 5:

Buy in Bulk Whenever Possible

$ $ $

*B*uying in bulk seems logical, but there are some basic tips to know in order to make it work. There are two ways to buy in bulk: large quantities of regular-sized items or large-sized containers. The best savings are earned with a combination of both.

Two examples of buying large quantities are when I buy a whole case of paper towels when they go on sale or several loaves of bread during my monthly visit to the day-old bread store. I calculate what I will use during one month and buy that amount. I say one month because that is approximately when an item is likely to go on sale somewhere else. If you can stock up for two months at a time, you will save even more.

Buying in large container sizes saves money because you are reducing the packaging and handling required by the manufacturer. It is really worth it to buy in bulk and deal with the minor inconvenience of repackaging the food into meal-sized bags or finding some storage space. Getting started may be difficult because of the cost involved. Eat very cheaply the first week, and use that savings to make your first bulk purchase. Each week will be easier.

A good example of this type of savings is boneless, skinless chicken breasts. Compare the prices of these different packaging types:

Chicken Breasts (boneless/skinless)
$4.99 per lb. Individual packages
$2.29 per lb. Warehouse club bulk
$1.99 per lb. Good sale
$1.79 per lb. Great (rare) sale

Ask friends and neighbors if they know someone who works at a meat distribution company, where you could buy meat wholesale. If this is unavailable, ask your butcher or meat department how much ground beef or turkey you would have to buy in order to get a discount. It might be forty pounds or more. Don't laugh— the price is worth it. The lean hamburger that would cost more than $2 per pound will be $0.99 per lb. if you buy a large quantity. The ground turkey that is usually $1.39 per lb. will be $0.69 per lb.

Some people don't like the quality or fat content of the cheaper hamburger. That's reasonable. I use the cheaper hamburger in recipes where the meat's flavor is obscured, such as meat for tacos, spaghetti sauce, or casseroles. For the recipes where the hamburger is featured more prominently, I buy the better grade meat.

Believe it or not, you can handle all of that meat at one time. Form some of the meat into meatballs and freeze them in plastic bags (each bag is a meal portion); make a huge kettle of chili and freeze it in meal-sized portions; and pack the rest of the hamburger in one- or two-pound portions and freeze individually for later use. You can ask friends if they want to join with you in a purchase. My friend had to buy eighty pounds of ground beef to obtain a good price. We split it among four families. I didn't have an extra freezer, and I could still store it with ease. Another benefit of bulk buying is that it helps avoid running out of something and having to rush to the store to pay full price.

Some of you say you can't buy in bulk because you don't have the space. I lived in a small townhouse with no storage space. I figured out how to use the little space that I had. I used old bookshelves in the garage for a pantry. I don't want an extra freezer because of the extra cost (both the initial cost as well as the extra utility expense), so I went to the local hardware store and bought a plastic-coated wire rack and put it in my tiny freezer above the refrigerator. The added shelf doubled the amount of useable freezer space. I know of people who store canned goods under beds or in hallway cupboards. I haven't had to go that far. But if you are motivated, you will be amazed at the storage space you can find.

CONTAINERS

I don't spend money on expensive storage containers. To maximize freezer space, I store my meals and food in plastic bags. When filled with a meal and flattened, the bags lie only a half-inch thick. I am able to stack several of them on top of each other. Once frozen, they can be turned sideways and stacked like books. If I used plastic boxes, I would not be able to fit many meals in my little freezer.

The cost of these bags is minimal. I pay between one and two cents per bag by watching sales and using a coupon at the same time. I use thirty per month for main meals (that's about fifty cents per month). I can wash many of them for reuse (I don't wash or reuse ones used for raw meat, eggs, or fish).

After World War II, people started demanding convenience foods. With this change, we have lost some of the wisdom of homemade foods and storage that our grandparents learned. People who went through the Great Depression let nothing go to waste. Food containers were saved. Everything was put to a new use. Even the flour sacks were used to make dresses (the material was soft cotton with a floral print). Here are some of the things we can glean from their experiences:

- Save jars (mayonnaise, syrup, etc.). Reuse them for your homemade syrups, chocolate sauces, salad dressings, etc.
- Save cardboard oatmeal boxes as storage containers for dry goods (your homemade granola, bulk items bought from bins, or small toys).
- Save cereal boxes for magazine holders (cut the side off diagonally and cover with Contact paper to make more attractive).

- Use Pringles cans to ship cookies to friends. The cans reduce breakage.
- Wash out plastic mustard squeeze bottles and fill with home-made colored frosting for cake and cookie decorating.
- Reuse margarine tubs for food storage. The largest sizes available (usually five pounds) are large enough to store food for one meal. The smaller containers are good for leftovers, lunches, and side dishes.
- Reuse resealable freezer bags by washing carefully and then checking for leaks. Again, don't reuse bags that were used for raw meat, raw unshelled eggs, or fish.

CHAPTER EIGHT

GUIDELINE 6:

Make Your Own Whenever Possible

$ $ $

*M*ake your own" has been one of the most exciting of the eleven guidelines, a never-ending exploration with great rewards.

Most people believe they have to *buy* everything they need. It wasn't that long ago that we *made* everything we needed. People even made their own baking powder. Recipes for just about everything you use can be found in some cookbook. The older the book the better. Garage sales and libraries are great sources for these cookbooks. One of my favorite newer cookbooks is the *More-With-Less Cookbook* by Doris Longacre. This is full of recipes for simple homemade alternatives to common grocery items such as cereals, soups, breads, etc.

Depending on your source for homemade alternatives, making your own can save you more than pocket change. Some people enjoy the homey feeling that comes from cooking from scratch. If you do, then you'll benefit in more than one way from this advice. There are a few things that are cheaper to buy than make. I make my own only if it will save money or if it will be more nutritious.

To get the most from my time in the kitchen, I looked at my spending and attacked the highest expenditures first. I reviewed four weeks' worth of grocery receipts and categorized my expenditures by food type (dairy, breakfast, meat, vegetables, snacks). I picked the most expensive type and went to work, creatively replacing premade foods with homemade alternatives. Below are the types of food I began making instead of buying. They are in order, starting with those for which we spent the most, ending with those for which we spent the least.

BREAKFAST

My highest expense was breakfast. We spent $40 per month on this one meal—and that was in 1992. Most homes spend 25 to 30 percent of their food bill on breakfast products, relying on prepackaged cereal for this meal. We did too. This has become a very profitable business for the manufacturers. The average box of cereal costs $3.50 to $5. Many families eat two or three boxes per week. That's $40 to $60 per month just for cereal. This is a worthy target for the miserly arrow.

My first move was to introduce alternatives to cereal two to three times per week. I don't slave in the kitchen every morning. Once a month or so I make a double batch of muffins, banana bread, or pancakes, and freeze them. It's so easy to pop the frozen item in the toaster oven or microwave for a meal.

Don't use prepackaged baking mixes. You will lose your savings on them. Baking from scratch takes about the same amount of time as using a baking mix. If you're addicted to these, make your own baking mix. Mixes can be stored for up to six months without refrigeration. They can be used with any Bisquick recipe you have. Here's my favorite:

Baking Mix

8 C. flour
1¼ C. nonfat dry milk powder
¼ C. baking powder
1 T. salt
2 C. shortening

Combine flour, milk, baking powder, and salt in a very large bowl. Cut in shortening until it resembles coarse cornmeal. Store in tightly closed covered container in a cool place (cupboards are fine). Makes about 10 cups.

I then experimented with recipes for cereal. I found one for Grape Nuts, several for granola, and some for muesli-style cereal. (See chapter 15, "Some Great Recipes," for my husband's favorite granola recipe.) All were delicious and cost only a fraction of the price of store-bought versions (remember that the manufacturers have to pay for all that glitzy advertising). I occasionally buy boxed cereal when it is on a good sale, combined with a coupon. This way I only pay $1 to $2 for a box. With these changes, I reduced my breakfast spending to $20 per month. That's half! To show what a difference cooking from scratch can make, here are some cost comparisons:

Sample of Cost Comparisons

Breakfast food	Name brand	Homemade
Granola (1 lb.)	$2.89	$1.00
Pancake syrup (24 oz.)	3.69	.25
Frozen microwave pancakes/ waffles (12)	1.89	.35

SNACK FOODS AND DRINKS

My next highest expense was snack foods, which includes cookies, chips, fruit leather, candy, Popsicles, ice cream, and beverages. My first move was to try to introduce a homemade treat whenever a snack was needed. Candy and chips can be replaced with homemade cookies or homemade granola bars.

Popsicles bought at the store cost more than homemade and usually have additives you may prefer to avoid. Making them at home also is a great way to use yogurt and fruit that might spoil if left unused. Here are some ideas:

- Puree fruits that are getting a bit mushy or overripe in a blender. This works well with watermelon, strawberries, and bananas. Fill Popsicle molds.
- Mix plain yogurt with fruit juice or fruit extract and a bit of

sugar to taste. Pour in Popsicle molds. This is only a good buy if the yogurt is on sale or needs to be used soon.

Soda can be replaced by generic versions of Kool-Aid or other drink mixes. We even suggest the kids drink water when they are thirsty, since that is what their bodies need. When frozen concentrated juices go on sale, we buy several. We still need to control how much of these are used up in a week. If we don't, we tend to drink up in a week what was bought to last for a month. One way to "ration" the good drinks is to only allow one cup of juice at meals and water after that if someone is still thirsty. Another is to only allow water at mealtimes and juice after the food is finished. This way they don't fill up on the drinks and skimp on the food.

The average household consumes sixteen quarts of soft drinks or juices per month (two bottles of two-liter sodas per week). If we calculate the cost over one month for each of these, it really adds up: some people spend $30 per month on beverages alone. Next to water, it is much cheaper (up to ten times cheaper!) to serve instant drink mixes than sodas.

For a special snack, we make a smoothie. We put some fruit in a blender (strawberries, peaches, bananas, kiwi, oranges, or whatever we have on hand) and add some liquid (apple juice or milk) and blend until smooth. For a thicker texture, add ice or frozen fruit, replace the milk with yogurt, and blend. It's refreshing, healthy, yummy, and inexpensive (the gourmet shops sell these for $3 to $5 each).

Another snack we frequently make are cookies. We enjoy making them together (and eating them together). Most people buy their cookies. I have heard many people talking in stores, saying that you can't make your own any cheaper than the packaged cookies, especially when they are on sale. I often wondered if this was really true. So I took out my calculator (again) and figured the cost for chocolate chip cookies. Homemade cookies usually cost half that of premade versions.

The most expensive ingredient is the chocolate chips, which I buy when on sale. Other types of cookies are less expensive, such as oatmeal or snickerdoodles. To save time, I make a double or triple batch of cookie dough. I divide the dough into balls the size of a baseball and freeze each ball. Or leave in the refrigerator for up to one week. When it's baking time, I thaw one ball and bake the cookies. This way my cookies are always fresh when wanted.

$\mathcal{M}$EATS

Another high expense for many families is meat. I cut meat costs in three ways: buy it in bulk, "stretch" it, and replace it with nutritious alternatives.

A few years ago I read about a woman who had a target price for meat of $1 per pound. I laughed when I read this and wondered how I could ever share that goal. Then I began to watch the ads. Hamburger occasionally goes on sale for $0.99 per pound (in bulk packaging). I buy these and slice them into one-pound portions and freeze them. When you need a pound, pull one out. Then I saw ground turkey go on sale for $0.79 a pound. Scan the sale flyers each week. I have seen pork roast for as little as $0.68 a pound and country-style ribs for $0.99 per pound.

For leaner meat, buy a roast on sale and have it ground. You can also go in with a few friends and buy the higher-grade meats in bulk from your butcher or meat department at a good discount.

At Thanksgiving many stores offer a lower price on turkey during the few days before that feasting Thursday. I can usually buy a turkey for $0.29 per pound. Stock up with as many as your freezer can handle. I try to buy as large a bird as I can fit into my oven. I then have leftovers for a week or more at very little cost or effort. After we eat our Thanksgiving meal, I cut the meat off of the bone and freeze meal-sized portions. I use the best cuts for turkey sandwiches or turkey fillets. As the week progresses, I serve the smaller pieces in stir-fry or Creole-type dishes. When I get down to the bone, I make soup. Nothing goes to waste. Here are some turkey buying and cooking tips to assist you:

- Plan on one pound of turkey per person. This does not allow for leftovers, however.
- A tom is the male turkey and is usually tougher (but larger). A hen is the female and is usually smaller and more tender.
- To thaw a turkey in the refrigerator, plan ahead. Thawing takes about twenty-four hours for every five pounds of turkey.

- To thaw a bird in the sink, cover with cold water and allow approximately twelve hours for large birds and approximately five hours for smaller ones. Remember to change the water often, keeping it cold.
- Many cookbooks recommend roasting turkey breast-side up. I prefer to roast my birds breast-side down. This allows the juices to run down into the breast, making the meat more tender and juicy.
- Loosely cover the top of the bird with foil. This keeps it from browning too much and drying out.
- Don't keep opening the oven to peek at the bird. You let heat escape each time and lengthen the baking time.
- For a gourmet touch, rub the skin with half of an orange. Do this close to the end of the roasting or it will burn.

Stretching your meat is a good way to reduce expenses. Adding a filler stretches the meat's volume, while keeping its nutritional value and flavor. Two fillers that work well and are nutritious are boiled wheat kernels and TVP. Boiled wheat is simply whole wheat kernels (found at health food stores and some grocery stores) that have been boiled until soft. TVP is a soy product that looks and feels like ground beef but has no flavor. It assumes the flavor of the seasonings you add. It is dried and is reconstituted by mixing equal parts of hot water and TVP. Both fillers are low in fat, inexpensive (each costs around forty cents a pound) and high in fiber. Whichever filler you choose, use an equal amount of filler to hamburger. One family keeps a container of boiled wheat kernels in their refrigerator ready for any meal preparation.

Another way we beat the high cost of meat is by replacing meat with vegetables, grains, legumes, or beans. This will lower your fat intake and help you with your "five-a-day" consumption (nutritional guidelines recommend at least five servings of fruits and vegetables per day). By using healthy alternative all-grain recipes, you can feed a family of four for one dollar. I have even found several lentil-rice, veggie burger, and rice and bean recipes that my picky eaters like. I am not suggesting you become a vegetarian. Rather, I recommend that you replace a few meals per week with a non-meat or low-meat dish. Some ideas are stir-fry, egg and rice casseroles, and potato-based dishes.

Eggs are another way to fulfill your protein needs, but for less money than meat. Eggs cost six to eight cents each when on sale. A quiche dish for four requires four to six eggs plus a few other ingredients and costs about one dollar. Other egg-based dishes that are low-cost are frittata, soufflé, egg salad sandwiches, fried rice with egg, egg drop soup, and omelets (yes, it's okay to eat them for dinner). As I mentioned in a previous chapter, eggs freeze well when taken out of the shell. So buy them in bulk when on sale.

Here is a price comparison list of meat alternatives:

- steak dinner for four = $8 to $10
- fish fillets for four = $8
- hamburger dinner for four = $5
- stir-fry dinner for four = $3 to $4
- rice and beans for four = $1.50
- quiche for four = $1
- lentil-rice casserole for four = $1

For more information on meat alternatives, please read chapter 10, "Cut Back on Meats."

PRODUCE

The last high expense I noticed was produce. While you don't want to skimp on vegetables and fruit, there are ways to reduce their costs. Supermarkets make 30 percent of their overall profit from their produce section. Once I learned this, I knew there had to be cheaper ways to buy fresh produce.

The first way to save money is to grow your own. If you have yard space that isn't being used, make it work for you (instead of you working for it by mowing, weeding, etc.). I have a friend who converted her lawn into a huge vegetable garden. She doesn't buy much produce anymore. When you grow your own, the vegetables cost about one cent each. For more information on how to set up a productive garden for little money, see chapter 17, "Stretch the Season."

The next best thing I did was take advantage of the farmers' markets. The prices are great! Much of the produce is organic as well as very fresh. Most of the items are allowed to vine-ripen, making them more nutritious. Go at the end of the day and get even better savings. Many farmers don't want to take anything back home with them and are willing to sell cheaply. If you are able to can or freeze, buy extra vegetables and fruit. You'll have plenty of produce on hand, and you'll be able to beat the high off-season prices at the supermarkets. Below is a list of what's commonly found "in season" at a farmers' market. Your region may not have all of these. Since things are cheaper when they are in season, plan your menus around in-season foods and reduce the cost of your meals.

Seasonal Produce Savings

Summer: grapes, lettuce, tomatoes, plums, avocadoes, zucchini, peaches, melons
Fall: apples, winter squash, oranges, pumpkins, broccoli, melons
Winter: broccoli, oranges, acorn squash
Spring: berries, asparagus, bananas, plums
Year round: potatoes, carrots, celery

If you can't get to a farmers' market, the next best thing is to stock up on fresh or frozen vegetables on sale. One local grocery chain has an annual ten-cent sale on produce. This is a great way to get your five-a-day. I stock up on whatever is being sold, freezing the produce for future use. Since some produce needs preparation before freezing, consult the experts. There are some suggested books on this topic at the end of this chapter.

It's best to eat fresh produce to obtain the right nutrients. But unless you grow your own or buy organic produce, frozen vegetables can be as healthy as fresh. Produce from supermarkets are not as full of nutrients as we would hope. First, they have been picked one to three weeks before they ripen, so they have less nutrients than a vine-ripened equivalent. Then they have been washed and bathed in water mist for one to two weeks at the stores to look appealing, which can cause nutrients to leach out. The saddest part is that they have been bred in order to look a certain way, and many of the nutrients have been bred out of them as well. All of this explains why a frozen vegetable is no worse than a "fresh" one in the stores. The frozen one actually might have more nutrients because it hasn't been sitting around in a store for a week or more. They are fast frozen and bagged without being cooked.

The last and least desirable way to save on produce is to buy canned fruits and vegetables. We don't do this too often, since the canned produce has been cooked and salted, often leaving less nutrients than fresh produce. Many nutrients are heat sensitive, getting lost in the long cooking process of canning. According to Jean Carper in her book *Food—Your Miracle Medicine* (Harper-Collins, 1993), we should eat both raw and cooked vegetables, but the vegetables should be *lightly* cooked (not stewed or boiled). Eating canned fruits and vegetables occasionally won't hurt us and can be a welcome financial boost. I have found that canned vegetables and fruits are sometimes cheaper than fresh or frozen versions.

Don't forget that fruit and vegetable juices can help us reach our five-a-day goal too. These are helpful in the winter months when there is less variety of fresh produce available. Fruit juice in the morning and a mixed vegetable juice as a snack are very healthy.

Cooking Tip: A good way to cook vegetables is in the microwave—with only a teaspoon of water or none at all. All of the nutrients stay in the vegetables and they retain a good texture and color.

SPECIALTY FOOD ITEMS

With the health craze increasing the consumption of low-fat and low-cholesterol foods, we sometimes think we have to buy these items in order to eat healthy. We need to keep this in perspective. (We also must remember that just because something is fat-free doesn't always mean it's good for you.) The marketing folks at the food manufacturers know this too. Have you noticed the re-labeling on many foods? Hershey's Chocolate Syrup now claims to be fat-free. It always has been. Again, all we need to do is learn to cook with less fat. Here are some tips I have learned to make low-fat treats.

Fat Substitute Chart

To lower the fat content in:	*Replace with equal amounts of:*
cakes, cookies, and breads	applesauce
chocolate cake, cookies, brown-ies	pureed prunes (baby food works well)
sauces and dressings	nonfat yogurt
mayonnaise or sour cream	nonfat yogurt

*L*UNCHES

Many folks struggle with how to provide a healthy lunch for the kids (or hubby) that can travel in a lunch box. Whenever I need to pack a lunch, I try one of the ideas listed below. Whether you use these ideas or others, try to include the following several times per week: fruits, vegetables, grain products (especially whole-grain types), lean meat or alternates (dry beans, peas, lentils, peanuts, and eggs), and low-fat milk, cheese, or yogurt.

Main Dishes:

- tuna fish sandwich
- egg salad
- ants on a log (celery stick with peanut butter and raisins on top)
- bagel and cream cheese
- lunchmeat sandwich
- peanut butter and jelly sandwich
- soup in a small thermos with crackers or cornbread
- cold pasta salad with whatever you like (olives, cheese chunks, celery, tofu pieces)
- leftovers
- black beans spread on whole wheat bread
- tortilla rolled up with shredded carrot and a turkey slice
- burritos (see page 74 for tips on burritos)
- risotto mixed with vegetables, and a green salad
- cheese enchiladas and rice
- tofu stir-fry and fresh fruit
- chicken salad with crackers

- homemade pizza and bread sticks
- cold barbecued chicken
- cheese and crackers and fresh fruit
- hamburger
- hot dog
- sloppy joes (pack bun separately)
- baked beans in thermos
- spaghetti or goulash
- stir-fry with rice

Snacks:

- homemade granola bars
- muffins
- homemade cookies
- carrot or celery sticks
- homemade pudding, gelatin, or rice pudding
- fruit
- applesauce
- zucchini or banana bread
- graham crackers
- pudding (make it from a mix and put in a thermos)
- snack mix (pretzels, unsalted peanuts, raisins, sunflower seeds)
- popcorn with spices (chili powder, taco seasoning, Lawry's seasoning, cheese powder)
- something to dip (use small containers for dip):
  pretzel sticks and peanut butter; bread sticks and low-fat Cheez Whiz; tortilla chips and salsa; vegetables and ranch dressing.

The key is to pack these in your own containers and not buy the prepackaged individual-sized servings. Invest in a wide-mouthed thermos to keep hot foods warm and an insulated lunch box or bag to keep cold things cold.

Drinks:

Buy a small thermos and fill it with juices, homemade lemon-ade, or milk. Avoid the prepackaged juice boxes or small cans.

Miserly MOMS

They cost twice as much as filling a thermos from a larger-sized juice container. Make your own juice from frozen concentrate and save up to three times the cost. This is true even when comparing name-brand frozen juice to its prepared and bottled equal. Make lunch box juices by reusing small water bottles and filling with juice.

Avoid "ades" or "punches." These just add sugar water to your drink and cost too much. Stick to 100 percent fruit juices. Try making your own drinks: Vegetable juice and fruit juice mixed (equal parts of orange and tomato juice); fruit juice cooler (unsweetened fruit juice and club soda).

Lunch Box Tips to Make It Work

Invest in a small freezer pack that can keep any perishable dish cold. Or, instead of buying an ice pack, fill a water bottle. Freeze it the night before and pack it with the lunch in the morning. It will be thawed enough to drink at lunchtime and keeps the food cold.

Leftover Tip

If you make enough at dinnertime to have leftovers, but your family eats everything you put on the table, try this tip. After the meal is made, but before you serve it, set aside enough for lunches. What they don't see they won't miss. Leftover lunches can save $1,000 to $2,000 per year.

Burritos and More

Make inexpensive burritos by layering refried beans, Spanish rice, and cheese on flour tortillas. Make your own Spanish rice by mixing rice with some seasoned canned tomatoes. Avoid instant rice; it costs more. Buy the flour tortillas, refried beans, and cheese in bulk. You can make thirty or more burritos in assembly-line fashion in little time. Wrap each one in plastic wrap and freeze. They make a great snack or lunch box idea. If a microwave isn't available to reheat an item, warm it in the morning and pack it with a warmed insulating wrap or in a wide-mouthed thermos placed in an insulated lunch bag.

You can do this with peanut butter and jelly sandwiches, hot dogs, hamburgers, and breakfast sandwiches/burritos. Peanut butter and jelly sandwiches freeze well. Make several and freeze in Baggies. Hot dogs and hamburgers will taste best if grilled first (make a large batch). Freeze in a bun and warm to eat. The breakfast sandwich can be made ahead of time by combining a fried egg, a slice of American cheese, and a slice of ham with an English muffin. Wrap up tightly and freeze. Reheat when ready to eat.

Make It Appealing

Kids like small things. You can make your lunch box goodies more appealing for them: Cookies can be cut with smaller cookie cutters; brownies can be baked in mini-muffin tins. Cut sandwiches in four pieces. Use tiny plastic boxes to make it fun. This would be a one-time purchase of a couple of tiny boxes that can be reused all year.

Bread Boredom

Are they bored with the same old bread? Try these ideas to zip things up: cinnamon bread, French bread, multi-grain bread, raisin bread, cheese bread, rye bread, oatmeal bread, Boston brown bread, pumpernickel bread, herb bread, onion bread, potato bread, bran bread, pita bread, hot dog bun, English muffin, sub roll, hamburger bun, kaiser roll, bagel, hard roll, biscuit, tortillas, rice cakes, or crackers.

Nutrition

I have heard from many moms that they feel they need to purchase prepackaged lunch box meals in order to provide healthier, low-fat foods, and that being frugal and making the lunches means eating high-fat or high-starch meals. I want to take a minute to discuss this myth.

Making a homemade lunch doesn't mean it has to be high in fat or starch. Often you can replace the same item for a low-fat version. For example, buy chicken or turkey hot dogs instead of full beef, or buy the more expensive fat-free ones if you can. For macaroni and cheese, replace the milk with low-fat or nonfat milk and the butter with yogurt. For bagels and cream cheese, buy low-fat or nonfat cream cheese. Peanut butter is high in fat, but also high in protein. You don't need too much to meet a person's protein needs. Try all-natural peanut butter with no added oil. For the tuna and egg salads, you can replace the mayonnaise with low-fat or nonfat mayonnaise or yogurt. Disguising the taste with relish is helpful. Ham lunchmeat is usually as low in fat as turkey and can often be purchased more cheaply on sale or in bulk from warehouse clubs.

Snack foods don't have to be bread-based. They can be sliced vegetables, fruit, or even a fruit or green salad (with dressing on the side so it won't get soggy). The low-fat and nonfat versions of mayonnaise, yogurt, milk, salad dressings, etc. are not that different in price and can be bought on sale in the same manner as other items.

Staying within budget and keeping it healthy at lunch takes the same planning and forethought as other meals. You can do it.

RESOURCES

Better Than Store-Bought, Elizabeth Witty (Perennial Library, 1979).

Cheaper and Better: Homemade Alternatives to Store-Brought Goods, Nancy Birnes (Harper & Row Publishers, 1988), out of print; check library for copy.

Eat Healthy for $50 a Week: Feed Your Family Nutritious Delicious Meals for Less, Rhonda Barfield (Kensington Publishing, 1996).

Make-a-Mix, Karine Eliason (Fisher Books, 1995).

Make Your Own Groceries, Daphne Hartwig (Bobbs-Merrill, 1983), out of print; check library for copy.

More-With-Less Cookbook, Doris J. Longacre (Herald Press, 2000).

Not Just Beans: 50 Years of Frugal Family Favorites, Tawra J. Kellam (Not Just Beans, 1999).

The Use-It-Up Cookbook: A Guide for Minimizing Food Waste, Lois C. Willand (Practical Cookbooks, 1979).

Will It Freeze? An A to Z Guide to Foods That Freeze, Joan Hood (Charles Scribner's Sons, 1982), out of print; check library for copy.

For resources on vegetarian cooking, please visit the resource section in chapter 10, "Cut Back on Meats."

CHAPTER NINE

GUIDELINE 7:

Eliminate Convenience Foods

$ $ $

*C*onvenience foods have eaten up (no pun intended) many of my grocery dollars in the past. I have shopped when hungry, looked at those yummy-looking packages that say, "You can eat me now—without the fuss," and taken them home. I have smelled and tasted the samples available during peak shopping hours—and bought the item.

Convenience foods are just that—convenient. And you are going to pay for that convenience, sometimes more than you think. With some preplanning, making your own meals and snacks from scratch can cut way back on your food bill. In my price studies, this is what I found about the cost of convenience food:

- A restaurant meal costs six to ten times more than one made from scratch.
- A frozen meal costs four times more than one made from scratch.
- A prepackaged mix costs three times more than one made from scratch.
- Precut foods (ready salads, sliced carrots, shredded cheese) cost two times more than if you cut them yourself.

One of my favorite examples of paying for convenience comes from a woman who called asking for help with her budget. She had no idea why she was always short of money at the end of the month. After much discussion, we figured it out. Every morning on her way to work she stopped at Starbucks for a cup of coffee and a muffin. She didn't think it added up to anything. We calculated that she was spending $100 per month for that convenience.

By changing our lifestyle a bit, we can save a great deal. To get away from the need for convenience foods, there are a number of things we can do. The first is to *plan* your meals so the fancy packages and smells in the store don't influence you. Have a meal plan and specific shopping list and buy only what is on your list. And make sure you aren't hungry when you shop! Remember the marketing "tricks" store designers play and be smarter than the snares they devise. Stores bake items during peak shopping hours, arrange toys and attractive prepackaged meals at eye level, and place high-priced snack foods at the checkout counter. Say no to these impulse items.

The second thing we need to do is become comfortable with our *kitchen* (you know, that room with the refrigerator in it). Plan on spending a little more time there and learn to cook some things from scratch. When I was a guest on the *Gayle King* TV show, I made a sample shopping list for a guest. One item on the list was a block of cheese (instead of presliced cheese at the deli counter that would cost her $1.50 more *per pound*). Gayle asked, "But what do you do if you want a slice of cheese?" I told her she would have to take a knife and slice it! It's amazing what people have missed in their kitchen.

Third, but certainly not least, is to buy items you use often in *bulk*. This helps avoid the convenience items when you run out of your stock and rush to the store to get whatever will work in its place (but at a higher cost). If time is a problem for you, then cooking several meals ahead of time would be advantageous to you. I talk more about this later in the book, but I wanted to mention some important tips about cooking in advance. By doubling recipes and freezing half for another day, I am able to build up a reserve of meals in the freezer. This is homemade convenience food. You pull out a meal and stick it in the microwave or oven—

just like the one that is four times more expensive in the pretty box.

Having meals in the freezer also keeps us from being tempted by those costly last-minute meals. I often used to order a pizza ($20) when I was too tired to cook or didn't have time to thaw the meat or cook from scratch. Now I have a frozen meal conveniently waiting on days like that.

Eating out is something we also did when I was tired. But that really adds up quickly. The average family eats out four times per week, including dinners, lunches, or brunch. The national average for money spent eating out is $85 per week per family.

Even meals made at home, but using premade mixes, sauces, etc. are costly. The take-and-bake pizzas are cheaper than a baked and delivered one, but they are still four or five times more expensive than homemade. Let's compare a chicken-and-noodle dinner made from scratch with a prepackaged one purchased at a warehouse club.

Convenience Item	Cost	Homemade Item	Cost
Chicken breast (1 lb)	$1.99	Chicken breast (1 lb)	$1.99
Instant noodle mix	1.29	Noodles	.35
(sauce included in mix)	——	Homemade sauce	.10
Frozen vegetables	2.49	Home-frozen vegetables	.99
Total cost of meal	$5.77	Total cost of meal	$3.43

That's a savings of $2.34 for this meal alone. If most meals have this type of cost variation, think of the difference you can make over a month's time (ninety meals). You could save up to $210 per month!

The marketing of prepackaged mixes is deceptive as well. Many ads lead us to believe we are making a home-cooked meal when we use their package. This sly marketing ploy appeals to your instinct that homemade is better (and cheaper). Remember, if the manufacturer did anything to "help" you make that recipe, you are paying them for that help.

CHAPTER TEN

GUIDELINE 8:

Cut Back on Meats

$ $ $

$\mathcal{T}$his chapter may sound extreme to some readers. Eating meatless meals is a big step to take. Remember, this was one more way we found to save money. If it's too extreme, move on to the next guideline. Or try these ideas once in a while to help the budget a bit. Some people have mentioned that eating frugally shouldn't have to mean eating beans and tofu. It doesn't have to, but including them is the cheapest way. You'll never find meat for $0.40 per pound, but there is a meat alternative that cooks up like beef at that price. If meat is a must in your home, skip this chapter and just incorporate my tips in chapter 8, "Make Your Own Whenever Possible," on reducing *some* of your meat expenses.

I had two reasons for reducing the meat in my diet. My first was a monetary reason. Meats are a very expensive source of protein. They can range from $1 to $8 per pound. Dried beans are an excellent source of protein, carbohydrates, iron, thiamin, and fiber. They cost very little, averaging about $0.25 to $0.69 per pound. They can be added to many types of dishes and are filling as well.

My second reason for reducing meat in our diet was health. I knew we needed protein, but I knew there were more nutritious sources of protein. I also knew we ate more protein than we needed. Most adult Americans eat too much protein. Even though the recommended serving size is three ounces, the average serving for dinner is between eight and ten ounces of meat. Unless you are a growing child, or pregnant, you probably need about half that amount. But a plate looks a bit empty with a small cut of meat or chicken on it.

We are supposed to eat more vegetables and fruit than most of us are eating. Only 20 percent of Americans eat the recommended minimum serving of fruits and vegetables (five per day). By reducing our meat and stretching it with more vegetables and fruits, we can solve two problems at once. Dishes like stir-fry, fajitas, salads, stews, potpies, and casseroles call for many vegetables and grains with a smaller amount of meat. These cost less to prepare and are more nutritious. I also added more alternative proteins (dried beans, tofu, grains) to our diet. There are some very healthy meatless dishes that our family enjoys.

When I first cut down on meat, I wanted to make sure we were getting the protein and other nutrients we needed. I started my nutrient research with protein. I wanted enough, but not too much, since extra protein turns into fat. Who needs more fat?

I looked at the recommended daily needs for protein for each member of our family (available in most nutrition books) and added up the foods we usually ate to see if we were getting what we needed. We were and had some to spare. The average adult needs 60 grams of protein per day. The Recommended Dietary Allowance for protein is .80 grams per kilogram of body weight, or .36 grams per pound of body weight. So a 120-pound person would need 44 grams of protein, and a 180-pound person would need 65 grams of protein. People's need for protein increases (as much as three times) if they are ill, under stress, pregnant, or nursing. Please consult a doctor before altering your diet.

I researched the types of proteins that provide the most protein per pound, while still watching fat intake. Here is what I found:

Proteins in Food

Food Item	Quantity	Protein*	Fat
Hamburger 17% fat (lean)	3 oz. cooked	21 gm.†	17 gm.
Chicken breast, skinless	3 oz. cooked	27 gm.	4 gm.
Chicken dark meat, skinless	3 oz. cooked	27 gm.	6 gm.
Turkey breast, skinless	3 oz. cooked	27 gm.	9 gm.
Cod (and most fish)	3 oz. cooked	28 gm.	5 gm.
Tuna	3 oz.	8 gm.	7 gm.
Egg	1	6 gm.	4 gm.
Yogurt, nonfat	1 C.	8 gm.	0 gm.
Milk, nonfat	1 C.	8 gm.	0 gm.
Peanut butter	1 T.	4 gm.	8 gm.
Peanuts	½ C.	18 gm.	25 gm.
Hot dog	1	5 gm.	13 gm.
Brown rice	1 C. cooked	5 gm.	1 gm.
Tofu	4 oz.	10 gm.	4 gm.
Dried beans, lentils	1 C.	15 gm.	0 gm.

By looking at these figures, I realized we could easily meet our needs with milk, some cheese, and lots of grains. Meats could be served less frequently, as a treat. Most countries use meat as flavoring or to enhance a dish. Their plates are two-thirds filled with grains, vegetables, or fruit. Americans tend to feature the meat, and the rest is considered a "side dish."

I began serving smaller portions of meat at mealtimes, filling the plate with grains, vegetables, and fruits. I stretched the meat in dishes such as stir-fry, fajitas, rice and beans, etc. I sometimes tried meatless recipes. You can feed a family a steak dinner or lentil soup with whole grain rolls, and they will get the same amount of protein. But they won't cost the same.

Make sure your family is getting the complete protein they

---

*Please note that the protein and fat figures vary depending on the size of the item and how it is cooked. I also found that several nutrition books had different protein and fat values listed.

†There is some debate over whether we assimilate all of the protein in meat or fish.

need from a meatless dish. A complete protein is the end result of two incomplete amino acids combining to form a complete protein. For example, rice is an incomplete protein, and beans are an incomplete protein, but when combined, they make a complete protein. Other examples of complete protein combinations are listed below.

According to nutrition experts, the key to making the combinations complete is making sure the grains are *whole* grains. Dr. Mauro Di Pasquale, Olympic medical committee member and author of *Amino Acids and Proteins for the Athlete* (CRC Press, 1997), states that we need to combine *whole* grains to make a complete protein combination. In other words, if we combine *white* rice with beans, it is not a complete protein—it needs to be brown rice. The same goes for whole wheat breads: they need to be 100 percent *whole* grain breads. Many manufacturers take out much of the wheat and replace a portion of it to add fiber or color. We need the entire kernel. Make sure the ingredient list includes 100 percent whole wheat flour. If it says simply says "whole wheat flour," it may, in fact, only be part of the wheat.

If you want to try a few meatless dishes, here are some guidelines to make sure you are getting the right combinations to form a complete protein.

Complete Protein Combinations

whole grains + legumes
whole grains + dairy
legumes + nuts or seeds
legumes + dairy
vegetables + legumes

Legumes are defined as a grain that is boiled or baked in order to be eaten. Some examples are chick-peas, mustard seeds, beans (kidney, lima, garbanzo, etc.), lentils, peanuts, and alfalfa.

Examples of some whole grains are amaranth, quinoa (pronounced keen-wa), millet, buckwheat, rice, rye, oats, wheat, barley, spelt, kamut, and corn.

Please note that nuts and grains do not form a complete protein. Also note that peanuts are not in the nut category, but are legumes.

Some examples of the above combinations are:

Whole Grains + Legumes
    lentil and rice casserole
    brown rice and beans
    pita bread and hummus
    beans with pasta (whole grain)
    baked beans and brown bread
    black-eyed peas and rice
    peanut butter and jelly on whole grain bread
    corn and lima beans (succotash)
    refried beans on whole grain tortilla
    falafel
    corn bread and pinto beans
    bean burrito on a corn tortilla
    oat muffins and soymilk

Whole Grains + Dairy
    rice and cheese
    whole wheat bread and cheese
    oatmeal and milk
    whole wheat macaroni and cheese
    whole wheat pizza with cheese
    refried beans with cheese
    rice pudding

Legumes + Nuts
    cashew and peanut butter sandwich
    bean and walnut salad
    couscous and pine nuts
    lentil and nut loaf

Legumes + Dairy
    beans and cheese
    lentil soup with yogurt
    yogurt with peanuts

Vegetables + Legumes
    bean and vegetable soup

cashew and vegetable stir-fry
eggplant and lentil casserole

How close together must foods be eaten to complement each other? From what I've read, most experts say complementary proteins don't have to be consumed in the same meal, but can be eaten within a few hours of each other or the same day.

My newfound zest for alternate sources of protein did not, however, cause me to become a complete vegetarian. Legumes and grains are a great source of most complete proteins, but some nutritionists teach that these combinations leave other elements lacking that can only be found in certain dairy, egg, or meat products. Some of these elements are choline, vitamin B–12, and vitamin D. This is why many legume dishes are combined with a small portion of cheese, meat, or eggs. If a person never eats an occasional meat, egg, dairy, or fish dish, some nutritionists suggest they might be deficient in these elements. I am not an expert on diet and am merely sharing my findings. I suggest you discuss these issues with a licensed dietitian before changing your diet and do some research on your own. Some books on the topic are listed at the end of this chapter.

Beans and tofu are an excellent way to stretch the budget. Here are a few tips on bean and tofu preparation. There are also some meatless recipes in chapter 15, "Some Great Recipes."

$\mathcal{D}$RIED BEAN PREPARATION SUGGESTIONS

One cup of dried beans will expand into two and one-half cups after cooking.

It is important to soak beans before cooking to reduce the amount of carbohydrates in the beans that cause gas, and to reduce cooking time.

Here are two methods for soaking beans before cooking. In both methods, first wash the beans and remove any beans that float when covered with water.

The overnight method

Cover the beans with cold water (four cups water to one cup beans) and let sit overnight. Drain, cover with water, and boil as directed.

The quick-soak method

Place the beans in a pot and cover with water. Boil for ten minutes. Remove from heat and cover. Allow to stand for one hour. Drain and rinse beans. Continue with your recipe.

Cooking times vary depending on the type of beans you are using.

- white (or navy) beans and soybeans require the longest cooking time—up to four hours.
- larger beans—two to three hours.
- smaller beans—one hour.
- lentils—one and one-half hours.
- lima beans—one-half hour.

Storage

Because beans require such long preparation and cooking time, cook several pounds of them and freeze in meal-sized bags. You can then drop the frozen bean portion into the cooking dish or soup. They will have a similar texture to canned beans.

$\mathcal{T}$OFU AND SOYBEAN PRODUCTS

Products made from the legume soybean (tofu, TVP, soymilk, and tempeh) are complete proteins and do not need to be combined with grains. They have zero cholesterol and are very inexpensive. They make a great money-saving meatless meal.

Soy products contain trace elements not found in any other plant. One example is choline, an essential element to the body. So far, it is only found in eggs, liver, and soybeans. Anyone avoiding all animal proteins should learn to incorporate tofu or other soybean products into their diet in order to be well balanced.

TVP stands for texturized vegetable protein, a food product made from soy flour. It comes in a dried form and needs to be rehydrated. It can be bought from local health food stores in several sizes, including granules (like ground beef), chunks (like chicken chunks), and patties (like chicken breasts). It has no flavor, so it needs to be seasoned. One ounce of TVP is equivalent to three ounces of meat. It costs about $.40 per pound when rehydrated. Once rehydrated, use it as you would its meat equivalent.

Tofu can also be very inexpensive ($0.99–1.59 per pound). It is even less expensive if you buy it directly from the tofu shops. These can be found in most Asian grocery stores. A great source of recipes for its use is *The TVP Cookbook* by Dorothy Bates.

Tofu is very bland and can be incorporated into any dish. We have made custard with soft tofu and used firm tofu in spaghetti sauces, sandwiches, stir-fries, and casseroles, in place of meat. It can be mixed with flour and spices to form a burger patty. Soft tofu can also replace any recipe that calls for cottage cheese, ricotta, or yogurt. When frozen and then thawed, it has the texture of ground beef. It takes on the flavor of whatever you add to it and is low in fat. The firmer the texture of the tofu, the higher the protein content. It has the same amount of calcium as milk. Most supermarkets carry it, making it easy to incorporate into your menus.

RESOURCES

Everyday Tofu: From Pancakes to Pizza, Gary Landgrebe (Crossing Press, 1999).

Recipes for a Small Planet: The Art and Science of High Protein Vegetarian Cookery, Ellen Buchman Ewald (Ballantine Books, 1973).

This Can't Be Tofu: 75 Recipes to Cook Something You Never Thought You Would—and Love Every Bite, Deborah Madison (Bantam Publishing, 2000).

365 Healthful Ways to Cook Tofu and Other Meat Alternatives, Robin Robertson (Plume, 1996).

The TVP Cookbook, Dorothy Bates (The Book Publishing Company, 1991).

The Vegetarian Way, Virginia Messina, M.P.H., R.D. and Mark Messina, Ph.D. (Harmony Books, 1996).

http://www.idiotsguides.com/Quick-Guides/MG—VegetarianBasics/file.htm. This article is a solid starting point for learning about the basics of vegetarian nutrition. Also includes references to other Web sites for further information.

http://www.vegparadise.com/basics.html. A Web site that defines what vegetarianism is, types of vegetarian diets, and how to begin a vegetarian regimen.

http://www.vrg.org/nutrition/protein.htm. Protein in the Vegan Diet (article), Reed Mangels, Ph.D., R.D.

CHAPTER ELEVEN

GUIDELINE 9:

Waste Nothing

$ $ $

$\mathcal{T}$he "waste nothing" mentality was prevalent in previous generations. Nothing was thrown out until it had been so used or recycled that it became useless for anything. Defining when something becomes useless varies from home to home.

Our grandparents were creative in finding uses for almost everything that came into their hands. Flour sacks were converted into dresses for the girls (the fabric was cotton with a floral print) and dish towels. I have an antique quilt hanging in my home that is filled with small squares of material from those flour sacks. Jars were reused to store homemade foods or small tools or bolts. Food that would be thrown out was fed to animals. Wood from broken crates was converted to furniture or toys. Old tires were cut and used to resole shoes. The list could go on because there was no end to their creativity and resourcefulness in recycling.

We are being raised in a "disposable" age. Our parents wanted us to have it easier than they did. But with this blessing we lost an art. We don't know how to stretch things. We expect things to be ready-made, and then we throw them out when we're done with them. Our generation is learning that there must be a better way. We can stretch things a bit further. We recycle our cans and plastics to avoid filling up the landfills needlessly. We reuse large food containers for storing dry goods or small toys. If the boxes are small enough, they can be used for diskette or cassette storage. Oatmeal containers make good small-toy storage or a toy in itself (see chapter 29, "Crafts for Kids"). The large laundry detergent jugs can be used to store baking mixes (wash very well first). Milk cartons can be used for bird feeders or freezer containers. See additional reuse ideas in chapter 7, "Buy in Bulk Whenever Possible."

We can apply this "reuse" mentality to our food as well. Many leftovers can be made into another meal. The ends of bread loaves can be saved in the freezer for croutons, stuffing, bread pudding, or bread crumbs. Fruit about to turn bad can be made into smoothie drinks, pudding, Popsicles, jam, or fruit breads. Bananas can be frozen in their skins until needed. Bits of vegetables and meats can go into a pot in the freezer to be used in soups, stews, potpies, enchiladas, or stir-fry meals. Soak limp celery in ice water for several hours to revitalize it or chop and freeze it for use in casseroles.

My favorite book on the subject of reusing foods is the *Use-It-Up Cookbook* by Lois Willand. It lists every food you may encounter in alphabetical order. Each section lists uses for that food, recipes, and storage tips. It is very valuable for stretching food.

There is no end to the ways we can recycle wisely. And there are many creative people out there who can teach us new ways to reuse items. If you would like some more creative ideas for reusing items, please visit your local library and look up these books (and whatever others you can find!):

RESOURCES

Don't Throw That Out! A Pennywise Parent's Guide to Creative Uses for Over 200 Household Items, Vicki Lansky (Book Peddlers, 1994).

Living More With Less, Doris Longacre (Herald Press, 2000).

Never Throw Out a Banana Again—and 364 Other Ways to Save Money at Home (Without Knocking Yourself Out), Darcie Sanders and Martha M. Bullen (Crown Trade Paperbacks, 1995).

Reclaim, Recycle, Reuse All-Natural Products to Help Save the Earth, Alan B. Hayes (Sally Milner Publishing, 1992).

Use-It-Up Cookbook: A Guide for Minimizing Food Waste, Lois Willand (Practical Cookbooks, 1979).

CHAPTER TWELVE

GUIDELINE 10:

Institute a Soup and Bread or Baked Potato Night

$ $ $

*H*aving soup and bread for dinner once each week helps us stay within our food budget. Soups are inexpensive to make (when made from scratch) and they are nutritious. There are such a variety of soups in the world; you could try a new one every week and never repeat a soup recipe all year. Each country has some well-known soups in its cuisine. They probably have soups often for the same reason we do—it's inexpensive.

Most soups contain vegetables, some stock, and a starch of some type (potato, noodles, rice, etc.). These are the ingredients for a healthy meal. Check in your cookbooks for some recipes to get you started. There are cold soups, spicy soups, thick ones, and thin ones. Just about anything your family likes can be found in a soup form.

I avoid soup mixes and canned soups because of the high costs as well as the fact that they are not as nutritious as homemade soups. The canned and dried mixes have been cooked to death, highly salted, and loaded with additives to keep them "fresh" for you. Soup and bread made from scratch usually cost me $2 for the four of us. The same meal made from canned soup and store-bought bread would run $6. To keep the cost down, I use leftover meat and vegetables that couldn't be used for anything else. I keep a bowl in the freezer for these leftovers. When the bowl is full, I can make soup or a stir-fry dish. Things that I might put in the bowl are a small leg of chicken that isn't enough for a lunch, vegetables left in the pan after dinner, or vegetables that will spoil if not used right away. Anything is usable for a stew, soup, or other dish. This is originally what soups and stews were—leftovers stretched into one more meal. If time is a real problem for you, try making your own instant soup mix and having it ready for dinnertime. I have included some ideas in this chapter on how to make a soup mix.

The type of bread I like to serve with my soups is usually homemade biscuits. I serve corn bread once in a while for variety. And I bake bread if I have time. There are so many simple biscuit recipes in cookbooks. They take almost no time to mix and bake. For biscuit variety, add sour cream or yogurt instead of milk to make them fluffier. Add grated cheese to make them richer. Add herbs (dill or thyme) to make them tastier. Be creative. For those with time constraints, make up a master baking mix (most cookbooks have one—mine is in chapter 8). With these, all you need to do at dinner is add shortening and milk. If you really hate to mix up biscuits, the only cheap alternative I have seen are the canned refrigerator rolls that go on sale for about 50¢ per can. They are full of preservatives but are a quick solution.

My kids were not excited about the idea of soup night. Yours may not be either. Start them with something you think they'll like, such as a potato and cheese soup. When it's blended together, it's rich and cheesy. If they like wontons, try a wonton soup. If they like beans, try a black bean soup. If they like noodles, try chicken noodle soup. If they like lentils, make lentil soup. Start slow. Kids will adapt if they know that's all there is for dinner.

To help you get started, here are some of my favorite soup recipes.

$\mathcal{S}$OUP RECIPES

Instant Cream Soup Mix

2 C. nonfat dry milk
¾ C. cornstarch
¼ C. instant chicken bouillon
1 tsp. onion powder
½ tsp. dried thyme
½ tsp. dried basil
¼ tsp. pepper

Combine these ingredients and store in an airtight container.

To use for soup, combine ⅓ cup of the mix and 1½ cups of water. Bring to a boil while stirring often. Add a vegetable for more flavor, such as diced celery (for cream of celery soup), or some sliced mushrooms (for cream of mushroom soup), or some diced broccoli (for cream of broccoli soup).

To use for any recipe calling for a can of cream of mushroom, chicken, or celery soup, add ⅓ cup of the mix to 1¼ cups of water. Boil for a few minutes, stirring often.

Quick Potato-Cheese Soup

1 C. leftover mashed potatoes
1 C. water
2 C. milk
½ C. grated cheese
1 onion, diced
1 tsp. salt
1 tsp. pepper
2 T. flour
1 T. butter

In a saucepan, melt butter and sauté the onion until light brown. Stir in the flour and salt and pepper. Stir, forming a roux paste. Add water, stirring constantly. When mixed, add the rest of the ingredients. Stir while it thickens and the cheese melts.

Tip: You can replace the potato in most recipes with a turnip, if desired. They require the same cooking time and have a similar texture.

Black Bean Soup

2 (15 oz.) cans black beans or 2 C. prepared beans
1 (15 oz.) can stewed tomatoes
1 can chicken broth
1 onion, chopped
1 garlic clove, crushed
salt and pepper
1 T. oregano
2 T. lime juice

Combine ingredients (except lime juice) in a large pan and simmer until cooked through. Add the lime juice after the soup is cooked. Serve with homemade rolls or rice.

My Mom's Best Pea Soup

2½ C. chicken broth
1 12 oz. package frozen peas, thawed or 1 cups cooked
    fresh peas
1 tsp. tarragon
1 tsp. salt
1 tsp. pepper
1 T. butter
1 T. flour
2 T. lemon juice
1 C. milk

Put broth, peas, and spices in a blender and blend until fairly smooth. It will be a bit chunky. In a pan, melt butter and add flour to form a paste. Pour the blender contents into the pan and bring to a boil. Boil, stirring occasionally, for ten minutes. Remove from heat and add lemon juice and milk.

Potatoes

If soup is absolutely out of the question, try a baked potato night. Potatoes go on sale regularly for 20¢ per pound (5 lb. bag for 99¢). Save the same leftovers in the freezer, but serve them as potato toppers. Add some grated cheese, diced tomatoes, diced leftover chicken, diced vegetables, and onions to the smorgasbord. Or take a baked potato, scoop out the center, mix the center with ground beef and taco spices, and re-stuff the potato. Potato night is another cheap meal idea that can be done instead of soup night.

RESOURCES

50 Chowders: One-Pot Meals: Clam, Corn, and Beyond, Jasper White (Scribner, 2000).

Joy of Cooking: All About Soups and Stews, Irma S. Rombauer, Marion Rombauer Becker, Ethan Becker (Scribner, 2000).

Potatoes, Jillian Powell (Raintree Steck-Vaughn, 1997).

Splendid Soups: Recipes and Master Techniques for Making the World's Best Soups, James Peterson (John Wiley, 2001).

CHAPTER THIRTEEN

GUIDELINE 11:

Cook Several Meals At Once and Freeze Them

$ $ $

*T*here have been many excellent books written on cooking and freezing meals in advance. Two of my favorite books on the subject are *Frozen Assets—How to Cook for a Day and Eat for a Month* by Deborah Taylor-Hough, and *Mega Cooking* by Jill Bond.

Both authors teach you how the system works. These ladies do a good job of explaining the whole concept of cooking monthly, and give you several sample menus and recipes to follow. Jill Bond also shows you how to convert your recipes into any bulk cooking plan—whether you want to cook for four or forty!

Both books share the same premise—the more you cook in bulk, the more you'll save. Both books explain how shopping and cooking in bulk will save you money and time in the kitchen. Cooking once a month takes between two and three days to do all of the shopping and food preparation for thirty days. With both plans, you are shopping and preparing food up to the baking stage. For the evening meal, you merely thaw and bake the meal. A few dishes are precooked and only require reheating. Both books also offer many recipes to try as well as train you how to think and cook in bulk.

Preparing meals in advance saves you money in several ways. It will reduce your grocery bill and energy bill and will save you time. The grocery bill will be less because you are able to buy foods in bulk. A five-pound package of hamburger or a ten-pound bag of potatoes is cheaper than buying the same in lesser quantities. You also will spend less since you will be in the store less often. You won't pick up those impulse items each time you walk down the aisles.

Having meals in the freezer also saves by reducing the impulse to eat out or to order a pizza. When you are running late, too tired to cook, or the family is complaining that there is nothing to eat, you can say, "Dinner's in the freezer." This can be very handy for busy families.

You also save energy costs by cooking in bulk. Cooking several items at once doesn't require more energy than just one dish would and reduces the stove's use threefold. Browning ten pounds of hamburger instead of browning each pound separately saves energy.

As for your time in the kitchen, it will be reduced considerably. Most of us spend an hour in the kitchen getting dinner ready. If all of the chopping and mixing is done ahead of time, and all that is required is reheating or popping something into the oven, consider how much more free time you will have. Wouldn't it be nice if all of the celery and onions were diced at once?

I usually recommend that people try cooking in bulk slowly. It can be a bit overwhelming to plan a month of shopping and slicing. To start, just double or triple tonight's meal and freeze the extra. Do the same tomorrow. And in a few days you will have two to three weeks of meals stocked up with no extra sweat or planning. The reason I suggest the slow approach is to let you adjust to the idea of buying, cooking, and storing in bulk. If I sent you off to try a four-month plan now, I think you'd close this book and forget it. A four-month plan will save you the most money, but first you need to learn how to plan and shop ahead. Once you do, you will be ready to tackle larger amounts of planning and cooking.

Storage Space

People say they can't cook in bulk because they don't have an extra freezer. As I've mentioned, I got rid of my extra freezer years ago when I learned it was consuming $15 to $20 per month in electricity. I figured I needed that money elsewhere.

I only have the small freezer above my refrigerator. I have no difficulty freezing meals in this small space. I even store foods bought in bulk, such as hamburger and chicken. To expand my freezer space, I cleared out all unnecessary items to make room for important things. I asked myself if it would be used soon, how much it was saving me, and could it be stored in the refrigerator instead? I then went to a hardware store and purchased a wire rack shelf for $3 that divided the freezer in half. This created more storage space.

My next step was to freeze in containers that used less space. A friend taught me that storing in large zippered freezer bags takes very little space. When filled with a meal and laid flat, it is only a half-inch thick. Ten can be stacked on top of each other, two stacks to a shelf. Plastic containers are too bulky to make my small space useful.

Some people have questioned the cost of my plastic bag usage and wonder if I am using up my savings. I don't believe that I am. By using sales and coupons, I pay a few cents per bag. Many can be washed and reused. If I used plastic boxes, I would need my extra freezer back to cook for more than two weeks at a time.

*F*OOD SAFETY

One main concern when freezing in bulk is food handling and long-term freezing. What foods are safe to freeze cooked or un-cooked, and how long is it safe to freeze them? I found some wonderful resources on these topics and have listed them at the end of this chapter. I also located some useful resource people to answer questions on food preparation and storage, listed on the next two pages:

Food Safety Hotlines

- **U.S. Department of Agriculture Meat and Poultry Hotline**
  www.fsis.usda.gov/oa/consedu.htm . . . . (800) 535–4555
  For meat and poultry handling and freezing guidelines. They can answer your question from 10 A.M.–4 P.M. EST, or you can hear automated answers 24 hours a day.

- **FDA Seafood Hotline**
  www.fda.gov . . . . (800) 332–4010
  Prerecorded messages and publications 24 hours per day. You can talk to staff members from 12–4 P.M. EST.

- **Safe Tables Our Priority (STOP)**
  www.stop-usa.org . . . . (800) 350-STOP
  This group provides information on food-borne illnesses, and referrals to doctors, support groups, and lawyers. This was formed by parents of E coli victims.

- **National Center for Nutrition and Dietetics**
  www.eatright.org . . . . (800) 366–1655
  Registered dietitians answer questions and provide referrals on nutrients in food, food safety, vegetarian diets, cholesterol, etc.

- **Milk Hotline**
  www.whymilk.com . . . . (800) 949–6455
  Recorded messages, publications, and recipes. Also a message center to have a registered dietitian call you back.

- **Land O' Lakes Holiday Bakeline**
  www.landolakesinc.com/OurCompany/ViewNewsRelease.cfm/ ArticleID 4 . . . . (800) 782–9606
  From November 1 to December 24 they will answer your baking questions. Callers receive a free holiday recipe booklet.

- **Butterball Turkey Hotline**
  www.butterball.com . . . . (800) 323–4848
  From November through December they will answer your turkey baking questions.

- **Weber Grill Line**
  http://webergrill.com/ . . . . (800) 474–5568

During the summer months, staff are available Monday through Friday, and prerecorded messages are available 24 hours a day to answer grilling questions.

- **Food and Drug Administration (FDA)**
  http://vm.cfsan.fda.gov/list.html . . . . (301) 443–3170
  Information on foods, drugs, cosmetics, etc. sold in interstate commerce.

RESOURCES

Frozen Assets—How to Cook for a Day and Eat for a Month, Deborah Taylor-Hough (Champion Press, 1998).

Mega Cooking: A Revolutionary New Plan for Quantity Cooking, Jill Bond (Cumberland House Publishing, 2000).

Once-a-Month Cooking, Mimi Wilson and Mary Beth Lagerborg (St. Martin's Press, 1999).

Will It Freeze? An A to Z Guide to Foods That Freeze, Joan Hood (Charles Scribner's Sons, 1982), out of print; check library for copy.

CHAPTER FOURTEEN

Special Needs

$ \quad $ $ \quad $ $

*T*here are many folks with special needs in their diet as a result of allergies or a chemical reaction to the additives in foods.

Children in particular react to some of the more than 5,000 additives in our foods. It's not surprising, since these additives are chemicals and not elements found in nature. Most additives are petroleum derivatives. Other people have allergies to items commonly found in prepared foods (such as corn or milk). In order to work around these elements, people must find alternatives to items normally purchased and taken for granted. For example, instead of buying the crackers (or whatever) that are on sale, only specific name brands can be eaten that are known not to have additives or a particular food ingredient. This can raise the price of your grocery bill.

We experienced this challenge a few years ago. Our son reacted to additives in food and in the air (perfumes, solvents, fumes, etc.). We needed to buy only foods that were additive-free. This did not mean I could only shop at health food stores. I found most of our needs at local stores. But it did mean that I could no longer pick up the generic brand or the weekly special. This put a big crimp in our penny-pinching ways. This new challenge required an even deeper adherence to the eleven guidelines for a miserly way of life.

I have had several people express doubt that they can eat

healthy and only spend half of what they usually spend for groceries. It can be done. When special needs must be taken into consideration, it takes even more planning and shopping than the
average miserly mom does. You can't just drop into a health food
store with your shopping list and expect to save money. Our new-
est challenge in shopping helped prove to others that it can be
done.

To keep within my grocery budget, I needed to plan even
more carefully. I could never fall back on a convenience food or
restaurant meal because my son couldn't eat the additives. This
alone was an incentive to stay true to my guidelines. I could never
say, "I'm too tired to cook from scratch" or "I'm too tired to
shop." Just any brand of food was not an option. I had to watch
all the local flyers for sales on the foods he could eat. I had to
shop at several stores in order to buy the brands or types of foods
within his dietary guidelines and still get them on sale. I used co-
ops for the items only available at costly health food stores.

I made even more of our own foods than when I first started
with the eleven guidelines. We ate less meat and poultry, replacing
them with dried bean, whole grain, or stir-fry meals. This reduced
our overall costs so I could afford the more expensive health food
products. We applied all of the eleven guidelines a bit more than
we had done before.

So when I hear people complain that it's too much work to
save money, I think back to when we didn't have this additive
problem. Reaching our financial goals was so much easier then.

But anyone can do it. There is help for this type of challenging
cooking and shopping; agencies and support groups have researched the additive topic. If you want help or more information
on the reactions commonly experienced by food additives, contact the Feingold Association: West Coast (909) 685-0924 or East
Coast (631) 369-9340 (*www.feingold.org*). They specialize in the reactions (medical, emotional, and physical) people have to additives. You would be amazed at the problems they have linked to
additives: asthma, bed-wetting, aggression, sleeplessness, etc. They
have cookbooks, shopping lists, and mail-order food addresses to
help make this problem easier to manage.

Whatever your special dietary need, the eleven guidelines can
help keep you within your budget. You might have to work harder

than most, or be a little more creative, but they will prove helpful for any situation.

RESOURCES

Why Can't My Child Behave? Jane Hersey (Pear Tree Press, 1999).
Why Your Child Is Hyperactive, Ben F. Feingold, M.D. (Random House, 1985).

CHAPTER FIFTEEN

Some Great Recipes

$ \qquad $ \qquad $

*T*o supplement chapter 8, "Make Your Own Whenever Possible," I have included a selection of helpful recipes. (For more recipes, please look for my new cookbook, *Miserly Meals*.) These are good in terms of flavor and nutrition as well as providing savings. After each recipe, I have provided a cost comparison analysis to show what your homemade version is saving you. My cost is based on my price goals.

*B*REAKFAST IDEAS

Pancakes

These are a great savings over cereal. The cheapest and tastiest recipe I have found is this one. To save time and energy, bake twice the amount you need and freeze them. They reheat well in the toaster or microwave.

2 eggs
2½ C. buttermilk or sour milk
1 tsp. baking soda
2½ C. flour
2 tsp. sugar
4 tsp. melted butter or vegetable oil
3 tsp. baking powder
1 tsp. salt

Beat together until smooth. Spoon onto greased hot griddle. Flip over when bubbles appear.

Cost Analysis (one dozen):
Homemade = $0.35   Frozen Microwave = $1.98
Purchased Mix = $0.95

Maple Syrup

Homemade syrup can be made as thick as store-bought by replacing half of the water with corn syrup. You may also add butter flavoring purchased from the store. Both of these will increase the cost.

2 C. sugar
1 C. water
1 tsp. maple extract

Bring water and sugar to a slow boil over low heat, stirring constantly. Remove from heat before it comes to a rolling boil (to keep crystals from forming). Add flavoring as it is cooling. Store in the refrigerator.

Cost Analysis (24 oz.):
Homemade = $0.20   Mrs. Butterworth's = $3.19

Cinnamon Rolls

These taste like the famous cinnamon rolls sold in malls.

Dough
1 T. dry yeast
1 C. warm milk
⅓ C. white sugar
½ C. soft butter
1 tsp. salt
2 eggs
4 C. flour

Dissolve yeast in warm milk. Add the rest of the ingredients and mix well. Knead into a ball or put in a bread machine on the dough setting. Let rise until double in size. When ready, roll out to about ¼-inch thick. Spread with filling as described on the next page.

Filling
   ¼ C. soft butter
   1 C. brown sugar
   3 T. cinnamon
Spread butter evenly on dough. Sprinkle sugar and cinnamon evenly over buttered dough. Roll up dough. Slice roll into 1-inch slices. Place on a greased pan. Let rise until double in size. Bake 10 minutes at 400°.

Icing
   ½ C. soft butter
   1½ C. powdered sugar
   1 oz. cream cheese
   2 T. whipping cream
   1 tsp. vanilla extract
   pinch of salt
Beat until fluffy. When rolls are hot, spread lots of icing on them.

Cost Analysis per roll (makes 16–18 rolls):
   Homemade = $0.45   Store-bought = $2.99

Nonfat Granola

   This is my husband's favorite breakfast cereal!
   5 C. quick-cooking oats
   ¾ C. brown sugar
   ⅓ C. concentrated apple juice
   ½ C. nonfat dry milk
   ⅓ C. honey
   2 T. cinnamon
   ½ tsp. salt
   ½ C. dried fruit
Mix sugar, juice, dry milk, and honey in saucepan and heat over medium heat only until sugar dissolves. Combine dry ingredients and fruit in mixing bowl. Pour sugar mixture slowly over dry mixture and blend well. Place on cookie sheet and bake at 375° for 10–20 minutes, stirring every 10 minutes.
Options: Be creative by adding peanuts, sunflower seeds,

coconut, sesame seeds, peanut butter, or whatever else your family enjoys.

Cost Analysis (1 pound):
Homemade = $1.00   Store-bought = $2.39

Snacks, Breads, and Drinks

Chocolate Syrup (a.k.a. Hershey's Chocolate Syrup)

1 C. cocoa powder (unsweetened)
2 C. sugar
¼ tsp. salt
1 C. cold water
1 T. vanilla

Combine cocoa and sugar and blend until all lumps of cocoa are gone. Add water and salt and mix well. Cook over medium heat, bringing it to a boil. Remove from heat once it boils. When cool, add vanilla (otherwise much of the flavor boils away).

Cost Analysis (30 oz.):
Homemade = $0.90   Store-bought = $1.89

Fruit Leather

Grind any fruit in the blender—berries work best. Don't add water unless the blender cannot function without it. Spread thinly on a plastic-wrap-lined cookie sheet. Place in oven at 250° overnight or leave the light bulb on if you have a gas stove with a pilot light. Or you can leave it outside in warm weather for 1–2 days, if it is covered with a screen to keep the bugs out. Peel and enjoy!

Cost Analysis (4 oz.):
Homemade = $0.60   Store-bought = $2.29

My Chewy Granola Bars

3 C. any granola
½ C. honey
⅓ C. chopped peanuts, other nuts, or chocolate chips
2 eggs

Combine well and press into a greased 8 × 8 baking pan. Bake at 350° for 20 minutes. Slice into bars after it cools.

Cost Analysis (12 bars):
Homemade = $2.50   Store-bought = $4.58

Soft Pretzels

  3½ C. flour
  2 T. sugar
  1 tsp. salt
  2 pkgs. (¼ oz.) or 4 tsp. dry yeast
  1 C. water
  1 T. shortening
  1 egg yolk
  1 T. water
  coarse salt

Mix 1 cup of the flour with the sugar, salt, and dry yeast. In a separate container, heat 1 cup water and shortening to 120°. Slowly add to the flour mixture. Beat well for 2 minutes. Add ½ cup more flour and beat again for 2 minutes. Stir in the rest of the flour. Knead for 5 minutes. Set in a greased bowl and let rise in a warm place for 40 minutes (or double in size). Punch down.

Divide the dough into 12 pieces, and roll each one into a long rope (18–20 inches). Shape into pretzels or other shapes. Place on a greased cookie sheet, and rest for 5 minutes. Mix egg yolk and 1 T. water. Brush on the pretzels, and sprinkle with the salt. Bake at 375° for 15 minutes.

Cost Analysis (12 soft pretzels):
Homemade = $0.75   Store-bought = $3.99

Oatmeal Bread

This is my favorite bread recipe.
2 pkgs. (¼ oz.) or 4 tsp. dry yeast
2 C. quick-cooking oats
6 C. bread flour
2 tsp. salt
½ C. brown sugar
½ C. honey
2 T. vegetable oil
1¼ C. warm water
1¼ C. warm milk

Dissolve yeast in water and add milk. Add sugar and honey and stir. Add the rest of the ingredients. Mix well. Knead for 5 minutes, then let rise to double in size. Punch down, then knead again. Let rise once more to double in size. Shape into two loaves and let rise to double again. Bake at 350° for 20 minutes.

Cost Analysis (2 loaves):
Homemade = $3.50   Store-bought = $5.38

Tortilla Roll-Ups

This is my favorite hors d'oeuvre recipe.
1 pkg. 8" flour tortillas
2 pkgs. cream cheese spread, salmon-flavored
1 small can diced black olives
½ red onion, diced finely

Spread salmon-flavored cream cheese over the surface of a tortilla. Sprinkle with olives and red onions. Roll up the tortilla as tightly as you can. Slice off sections (use a serrated knife for best results), about ½-inch thick. Lay them flat on a platter. They should look like pinwheels.

Cost Analysis (3 dozen):
Homemade = $6.00   Store-bought = $12.00

ᴅESSERTS

Funnel Cakes

2 beaten eggs
1½ C. milk
2 C. sifted flour
1 tsp. baking powder
½ tsp. salt
2 C. cooking oil

Combine eggs and milk. Sift flour, baking powder, and salt. Add to egg mixture and beat smooth. If it is too thick, add milk. If too thin, add flour. Heat oil to 360°. Pour ½ cup into funnel and drizzle into the oil, forming a circle with drizzles in the center. Fry until golden brown. Drain on paper towel and dust with powdered sugar.

Cost Analysis (each cake—makes 6–8):
  Homemade = $1.25   Store-bought = $4.99

Nonfat Brownies

½ C. flour, sifted
½ C. unsweetened cocoa powder
¼ tsp. salt
2 large eggs
1 C. granulated sugar
9 T. unsweetened applesauce
1 T. vanilla

Grease and flour an 8 × 8 square baking pan and set aside. Combine flour, cocoa, and salt. Mix well. In a separate bowl, whisk together eggs, sugar, applesauce, and vanilla. Stir in flour mixture until just blended. Do not over mix. Pour batter into prepared pan. Bake 25 minutes at 325° or until a toothpick inserted in center comes out clean. Cool at least 15 minutes before cutting.

Cost Analysis (1 dozen):
  Homemade = $1.29   Store-bought = $2.29

Spices, Mixes, and Sauces

Many mixes are simple combinations of spices you probably have in your cupboard. For example, spaghetti mixes seem to be popular. They cost up to $1.99 per bag. You can save that by making your own with a few ingredients.

There are also bulk spice mixes you can buy at warehouse clubs. These are a bargain (as cheap as homemade) if you use the spice often. Most spices last one year on the shelf. Here are some of my favorite mixtures that we use regularly.

Spaghetti Herb Mix

½ C. garlic powder
½ C. onion powder
½ C. dried oregano
3 T. dried basil
3 T. dried thyme
3 T. salt
2 T. sugar

Store in airtight container. Makes 10 servings or uses. To use, blend 16 oz. tomatoes with 4 T. of the mix.

Cost Analysis (4 T./1 pkg.):
Homemade = $0.41   Store-bought = $1.99

Taco Spice Mix

¼ C. red pepper flakes or chili powder
¼ C. ground cumin
¼ C. oregano
2 T. cayenne pepper
¼ C. garlic powder
¼ C. onion powder
3 T. salt

Makes 12 servings or uses. To use, add 2 tablespoons to one pound of ground meat. Mix well and then cook. For dips, add 2 tablespoons to 1 cup sour cream or yogurt.

Cost Analysis (2 T./1 pkg.):
Homemade = $0.32   Store-bought = $0.99

Buttermilk Salad Dressing

    3 garlic cloves, minced
    ¾ C. mayonnaise
    ½ C. buttermilk (or ½ C. milk + ½ tsp. vinegar)
    1 tsp. dried parsley flakes
    1 tsp. onion powder
    ½ tsp. salt
    ½ tsp. pepper

Combine ingredients and blend well until smooth. Chill for at least 30 minutes. Tastes best if chilled overnight before serving.

Cost Analysis (16 oz.):
  Homemade = $0.75   Store-bought = $2.99

The Best Bleu Cheese Dressing

    1 C. sour cream
    1 tsp. dry mustard
    1 T. black pepper
    1 T. vinegar
    ½ C. milk
    ½ tsp. salt
    ½ tsp. garlic powder
    1 tsp. Worcestershire sauce
    1⅓ C. mayonnaise
    4 oz. bleu cheese

Blend all ingredients (except bleu cheese) well. Add cheese in very small pieces and stir well. Chill for 24 hours before using for maximum flavor.

Low-fat alternative: replace sour cream with plain yogurt.

Cost Analysis (26 oz.):
  Homemade = $3.60   Store-bought = $8.00

Garlic Croutons

    2 T. butter
    ¼ C. olive oil
    2 large garlic cloves, pressed
    4 bread slices, cut into ¾-inch cubes

Melt the butter, olive oil, and garlic in saucepan. Place bread cubes in a large mixing bowl. Add butter mixture and mix well. Place on baking sheet and bake at 350° until bread is brown and crisp (20 minutes).

Cost Analysis (24 oz.):
Homemade = $0.75   Store-bought = $2.99

Barbecue Sauce

1 C. ketchup
1 tsp. salt
1 tsp. pepper
3 cloves garlic, crushed
¼ C. brown sugar
1 tsp. dry mustard (optional)
¼ C. vinegar (cider or wine)

Combine all ingredients in saucepan. Let simmer for 15 minutes.

Cost Analysis (12 oz.):
Homemade = $0.75   Store-bought = $2.69

Steak Sauce

1 C. ketchup
1 garlic clove, minced
⅓ C. chopped onion
¼ C. each lemon juice, water, Worcestershire sauce,
    and vinegar
2 T. soy sauce
2 T. packed dark brown sugar
1 T. prepared mustard

Combine the ingredients in a saucepan and boil. Reduce to a simmer and cook for 30 minutes. Refrigerate the leftovers.

Cost Analysis (12 oz.):
Homemade = $2.11   Store-bought = $3.99

MAIN DISHES

Many people have asked what my family eats for dinner. Most have assumed that we live on casseroles and noodles. We enjoy a variety of foods and flavors. I have found ways to make our favorites, but for less. I have selected a few of our favorites to share.

Pizza

Few of us make our own pizza anymore. Making one from scratch is easy and can cost significantly less than buying one. Here is my favorite recipe:

Dough

    1 C. warm water
    1 pkg. dry yeast, or 2 tsp.
    1 tsp. sugar
    3 C. white (or wheat) flour
    2 T. oil (preferably olive)
    1 tsp. salt

In a bowl mix the yeast, sugar, and water, stirring to dissolve the yeast. Let it rest 5 minutes. Add the other ingredients. Knead the dough on a floured board, adding more flour until it's not sticky. Place in a bowl and cover, letting it rise from five minutes to two hours, depending on the texture you would like. The longer you let it rise, the more bread-like the dough will become. Punch down the dough and shape into a large pizza crust.

Dough variations: Mix herbs into the dough. Add 1 T. oregano or dill and 1 tsp. garlic powder.

Topping

Top with any of these combinations and bake at 450° for 15 minutes:

- For a vegetarian pizza, top with tomatoes, marinated artichoke hearts, olives, onions, and bell peppers.
- Brush the dough with olive oil, then sprinkle with basil and oregano.
- Sprinkle with diced chicken, herbs, and a bit of mozzarella cheese.
- Spread pesto over the crust, then layer a thinly sliced zucchini

and a few tomatoes. Sprinkle with basil, salt, and pepper.

- Use Monterey jack cheese if mozzarella is not available or price prohibitive.

Cost of dish (serves 4): $0.75 (per crust)

Leftover-Bread Meal

3 C. dried bread (broken into cubes)
4 eggs
1 can (32 oz.) spinach
½ C. shredded cheese (any kind)
1 tsp. sage
1 tsp. thyme
1 tsp. garlic powder
½ onion, diced
1 tsp. salt

Let the bread dry by leaving it out overnight loosely covered with a dish towel. Break it up into a large mixing bowl. Add the rest of the ingredients. Mix well. Put into a greased loaf pan. Bake at 350° for 1 hour. Slice to serve.

Cost of dish (serves 4): $1.89

Poor Man's Steak

1 lb. ground beef or turkey
½ C. crushed saltine crackers
½ C. water
2 tsp. salt
1 tsp. pepper

Combine all of the ingredients in a bowl and mix well. Pat into thin patties and fry in an ungreased frying pan. Serve as they are, or add a sauce for variety.

Cost of dish (serves 4): $1.25

Potpie

1 C. liquid chicken broth
1 onion, diced
1 potato, peeled and cubed

2 carrots, peeled and cubed
3 ribs of celery, cubed
1 C. leftover cooked chicken, cubed
2 T. roux (1 T. butter + 1 T. flour, melted together)
1 tsp. sage
1 tsp. oregano
½ tsp. paprika
½ tsp. pepper

Combine all of the ingredients in a pan and stir over low heat until it begins to thicken. Put in a baking dish and spoon the crust (recipe below) on top. Bake at 375° for 45 minutes.

Quick Spooned-On Crust
1 C. flour
1½ tsp. baking powder
½ tsp. salt
1 C. milk
1 tsp. vinegar
½ T. melted butter
½ tsp. pepper

Combine ingredients and spoon over chicken.
Cost of dish (serves 4): $2.90

Messy Chicken

1 lb. chicken (about 4 legs with thighs)
Salt
2 T. oil
1 onion, finely chopped
2 cloves garlic, pressed
1 tsp. ground cinnamon
½ tsp. ground cloves
2 T. brown sugar
3 small yams or sweet potatoes (1 lb. total), peeled, cubed
1 tart green apple, peeled, cored, and diced
1 can (8 oz.) tomato sauce
½ C. chicken broth
2 T. apple cider vinegar

Sprinkle chicken lightly on all sides with salt. In a deep frying pan, brown chicken in the oil. Remove chicken and set aside. To the drippings in the pan add onion. Cook until golden. Add garlic, cinnamon, cloves, and brown sugar. Add the chicken, yams, apple, tomato sauce, and chicken broth. Simmer for 45 minutes. Remove chicken, yams, and apple to a serving dish. Stir vinegar into sauce. Heat and stir until sauce is thickened. Pour over chicken. Serve over rice.

Cost of dish (serves 6): $4.25

Fast-Food French Fries

My kids enjoy the taste of McDonald's fries, but I can't drop in a few times a week like we used to. So I learned how to make my fries taste like theirs.

2 C. warm water
⅓ C. sugar
2 large potatoes, cut in strips
Oil

Dissolve sugar in warm water. Place sliced potatoes in the water and let set for 15–30 minutes. Heat oil in a deep pan (enough to cover potatoes) to 350°. Dry off all visible water from potatoes and place in oil. Cook for one minute, then remove. This cooks the insides. Let oil return to 350°. Place potatoes back into the oil and cook until golden brown. Remove, drain, and salt to taste.

Cost of dish (serves 2–4): 40¢

Fajitas

   ½ lb. chicken breast (or beef strips), sliced
   ½ onion, sliced
   1 bell pepper, sliced
   3 cloves garlic, diced or mashed
   2 T. oil
   2 limes (or lemons), squeeze for juice
   1 tsp. chili powder
   ¼ tsp. ground cumin
   ½ tsp. salt
   ½ tsp. pepper
   6 large flour tortillas

Toss meat and ingredients (except tortillas) together and marinate for at least ½ hour (the longer the better). To cook, layer the chicken or beef and vegetables on a broiler pan and place in broiler for a few minutes, or until chicken is done. Discard juices. The meat can also be grilled over the barbecue or pan-fried. If pan-frying, add all of the vegetables and juices to the pan with the meat.

   Serve on flour tortillas and roll up like a burrito. For a fancier meal, garnish with guacamole, salsa, sour cream, lettuce, and/or grated cheese.

   Cost of meal (serves 4): $3.60

Indian Curry

   2 C. meat (can be leftover pieces of chicken, beef, or fish)
   5 T. butter
   ½ C. minced onion
   6 T. flour
   4½ tsp. curry powder
   1¼ tsp. salt
   1½ tsp. sugar
   ¼ tsp. ginger
   1 C. liquid chicken bouillon
   2 C. milk
   1 tsp. lemon juice
   1 C. diced apple

Melt butter. Add onion and cook until golden. Add the next

five ingredients and stir into a paste. Add bouillon and milk. Cook, stirring until thickened. Add meat, apple, and lemon juice before serving. Serve over brown rice.

Condiments for curry (if available):

- chutney
- raisins
- peanuts
- coconut
- pineapple
- hard-boiled eggs
- pickles (sweet)

Cost of meal (serves 4): $3.75

Chinese Pineapple Chicken

1 lb. chicken breast, diced
1 tsp. cornstarch
pepper
1 garlic clove
Oil
3 tsp. soy sauce
1 (8 oz.) can pineapple chunks
2 T. water
1 T. cornstarch

Mix chicken with 1 tsp. cornstarch, pepper, garlic clove, and 1 tsp. soy sauce. Fry chicken in a little oil until underdone. Add pineapple (save the juice for later). Simmer 3 minutes. Set aside. Mix 2 tsp. soy sauce, water, leftover pineapple juice, and 1 T. cornstarch. Add sauce to chicken in pan and cook until thick. Serve on rice.

Cost of dish (serves 4): $3.75

Sandy's Cheese Chile Relleno Puff

2 (4 oz.) cans whole green chilies
8 oz. Monterey jack cheese, shredded
6 eggs

¾ C. milk
1 T. flour
1 tsp. baking powder
½ tsp. garlic salt

Grease a small baking pan. Lay down the chilies and cover with 4 oz. jack cheese. Combine the rest of the ingredients and pour over chilies. Top with rest of cheese. Bake at 350° for 30 minutes or until firm.

Cost of dish (serves 4): $3.29

Leftover Chicken Italian Meal

1 (8 oz.) bag of pasta (bow-tie, macaroni, egg noodles)
1 lb. leftover cooked chicken, cubed
1 (15 oz.) can stewed tomatoes
1 T. vegetable oil (olive preferably)
1 garlic clove, crushed
1 tsp. oregano
1 tsp. thyme

Boil pasta until done. Drain. In a skillet, heat oil, garlic, and herbs. Toss in tomatoes and chicken. Heat thoroughly. Toss with pasta. Serve with salad. For variation, add frozen corn or diced potatoes to sauce.

Cost of dish (serves 4): $2.79

MEATLESS DISHES

Thai Noodle Meal

½ lb. pasta
1 C. diced vegetables (use leftovers—carrots, celery, peppers, broccoli)
½ C. chunky peanut butter
3 T. soy sauce
1 T. vinegar (wine, cider, or rice)
½ tsp. hot pepper flakes (or Tabasco sauce, or any hot seasoning mix)
½ C. water

Microwave the vegetables until just tender. Cook pasta and drain. Set aside. Mix the rest of the ingredients in a saucepan. Heat and stir until well mixed and warmed through. Toss with pasta. Serve with a salad.

Cost of dish (serves 4): $1.79

Anne's Squash Casserole

6–8 small zucchini, thinly sliced
2 eggs
1 pkg. saltines, crushed
Salt and pepper to taste
¼ C. grated cheddar cheese

Cook squash and drain. Mash with a fork. Stir in the eggs. Add enough saltines to absorb liquid. Bake at 325° for 45 minutes. Top with grated cheese.

Note: For a nondairy diet, replace the eggs and cheese with ¾ cup mashed tofu.

Cost of dish (serves 4): $2.99

Vegetarian Chili

1 T. oil
2 cloves garlic, minced
2 onions, chopped
2 (16 oz.) cans stewed tomatoes
2 (16 oz.) cans kidney beans or 2 C. prepared beans
2 green peppers, chopped
1 (6 oz.) can tomato paste
3–6 T. chili powder
1 T. cumin seeds or 1 tsp. ground cumin
1 tsp. dried oregano
1 tsp. salt
½ tsp. pepper

Combine oil, garlic, and onions in large pan. Heat until tender. Stir in the rest of the ingredients and simmer for 30 minutes. Serve with corn bread.

Cost of dish (serves 6–8): $3.60

My Favorite Vegetable Pancakes

    3 C. vegetables, grated or finely chopped
        (Use what you have or what's in season. For a nice flavor,
        use mushrooms, zucchini, and leek)
    1 C. potato, grated
    ½ onion, grated or diced
    4 eggs
    ½ to 1 C. bread crumbs (substitute saltines or flour)
    Salt and pepper to taste
    ½ C. grated cheese (cheddar adds best flavor,
        but any will do)

After grating the vegetables, let sit for 15–30 minutes. Drain the grated vegetables of all visible water. Add eggs and seasoning, then add bread crumbs until a dough forms. Add cheese and mix well. Form patties and fry in ungreased nonstick pan. You can use a regular pan, but it may require a bit of oil to reduce sticking.

    Serve with brown rice and a salad. For added zest, drizzle your favorite sauce over the pancakes (salsa, hollandaise, Dijon, tomato basil, etc.).

Cost of dish (serves 4–6): $3.25

Easy Microwave Lasagna

    8 lasagna noodles, uncooked
    4 C. (or 32 oz. jar) spaghetti sauce
    2 T. wine vinegar
    1 (16 oz.) can spinach + liquid
    16 oz. ricotta or cottage cheese
    1 egg
    1 tsp. pepper
    1 tsp. oregano
    1 tsp. granulated or dehydrated garlic
    1 C. grated mozzarella cheese

In one bowl, combine spaghetti sauce, vinegar, spinach, and the liquid from the can. In another bowl, combine ricotta, egg, and spices. In two 8 × 8 glass pans, spread ½ cup sauce on the bottom of each pan. Then take 2 uncooked noodles and break to fit across bottom of each pan. Spread ½ cup of egg mixture over noodles. Sprinkle a little cheese over the egg mixture. Cover with

½ cup spaghetti sauce. Repeat layers in the same order, ending with sauce on top. Cover with plastic wrap.

Cook one pan 30 minutes on medium power in the microwave. When done, let sit covered (for added flavor) while the other cooks.

Note: For a nondairy diet, replace the ricotta cheese and egg with 2⅓ cups (18 oz.) mashed tofu, and omit mozzarella cheese or use tofu cheese.

Cost of dish (serves 4): $5.10

Huevos Rancheros

1 T. vegetable oil
1 medium onion, diced
1 clove garlic, minced
1 can (15 oz.) stewed tomatoes
2 T. chili powder
1 T. oregano
6 eggs
½ C. grated cheddar or Monterey jack cheese

Heat oil in a skillet and sauté onions and garlic until tender. Add tomatoes and spices. Stir to combine. Add eggs into the sauce, leaving a bit of space between them. Do not break the yokes. Cover pan and simmer, so eggs will poach. When eggs are done, scatter cheese over the eggs and wait until it melts. Serve on rice.

Cost of dish (serves 4): $3.25

Beans and Rice

Rice

Prepare rice for four people. Add ½ cup salsa and stir before serving.

Beans

1 (32 oz.) can of pinto beans or 4 C. prepared beans
2 oz. Monterey jack cheese (grated)
1 T. vinegar (cider)
1 T. oil
3 green onions, diced
1 T. cayenne pepper

Put oil in a frying pan. Pour in beans. Mash beans with a fork. Add cheese. Heat, stirring constantly. When smooth, add vinegar and cayenne; stir and remove from heat. Garnish with green onions.

For a truly authentic meal, prepare salad using salsa as the dressing.

Cost of dish (serves 4): $2.25

White Beans and Tomatoes

1 lb. white beans (soaked overnight)
4 C. vegetable broth or water
2 bay leaves
1 onion, chopped
4 carrots, sliced
4 stalks celery, sliced
2 tsp. brown sugar
4 garlic cloves
7 C. tomatoes, chopped (or 3 16 oz. cans stewed)
¼ C. lemon juice

Combine broth, beans, and bay leaves in a large pot. Simmer for one hour. Drain half of the broth or water. Add rest of ingredients (except lemon juice) and return to a boil. Cook for 45 minutes, or until thick. Remove from heat and stir in lemon juice. For added flavor, let sit overnight in refrigerator. Reheat before serving.

Cost of dish (serves 4): $6.50

Terry's Lentil Rice Casserole

    3 C. water or vegetable broth
    ¾ C. lentils, uncooked
    ½ C. brown rice, uncooked
    1 onion, chopped
    1 T. dry basil
    1 T. oregano
    1 tsp. thyme
    1 tsp. garlic powder (or 2 crushed garlic cloves)
    1 T. vegetable seasoning spice
    1 T. salt
    ½ C. grated cheese, tofu cheese, or yogurt (optional)

Combine all ingredients except cheese in a casserole dish. Cover dish with foil. Bake at 300° for 2½ hours. Remove from heat and top with cheese or yogurt before serving.

Cost of dish (serves 4): $1.50

Bean Sandwich Spread

    1 (15 oz.) can beans (garbanzo, black, or pinto),
        drained and rinsed, or 2 C. prepared beans
    2 T. yogurt or tofu
    ½ tsp. chili powder
    2 T. onion, chopped
    1 T. lemon juice (if using black beans, lime juice is better)
    1 garlic clove, crushed

Place all ingredients in a blender and mix to desired consistency (or mash by hand in a bowl). Spread on pita pockets or whole wheat bread.

Cost of spread: $1.89

CHAPTER SIXTEEN

Be Wary of Warehouse Clubs

$ $ $

*W*arehouse clubs are large, plain, unattractive buildings filled with things we think we need. I know people who do 90 percent of their shopping at warehouse clubs, believing they're being thrifty. Unfortunately, warehouse clubs need to be used as carefully as grocery stores. Regardless of what you've heard, they don't have the lowest prices on everything.

These stores are actually private clubs. You pay an annual membership fee for the privilege of shopping there. Almost anyone can join through their credit union, professional club, employer, or by having a business license. Membership fees are fairly expensive—anywhere from $28 to $50 per year. These clubs have sprung up across the nation, with Costco and Sam's Club owning most of the stores.

Some frugal experts have claimed that these stores only make a profit by charging membership fees. I don't believe this is true. The membership fees help them but are not the only source of income. From what I have read, seen for myself by shopping around, and learned by talking to various employees of these stores, I believe these stores make their profits four ways: membership fees, low overhead (no-frills buildings and minimal staff), high-volume sales of special deals, and high markup on certain items.

Many of the products they sell are inexpensive. But even their prices can sometimes be beat by other retail stores. Sometimes they make a small amount of profit on each item but sell hundreds of thousands of them (at all stores combined), which add up to a healthy profit. Have you noticed that they often carry only one brand or type of an item? This is not because it's the best one available on the market. They obtain a good deal on a particular product and want to move it as quickly as possible. If they sold any other brand or model of that item, they would have extra inventory to carry, and that represents lost profit. This is true of most of their products: there is only one brand of non-chlorine bleach, one brand of bandage, one brand of vacuum cleaner, one phone/ fax machine, etc. This is true of their grocery items as well. There are only a few brands available of each food type.

After comparing prices of many like items at our local warehouse clubs with local grocery store prices, I have shortened the list of what I buy at warehouse clubs to only ten or fifteen items. This list changes as they change their prices.

Many of the warehouse club bulk packages are the same price as individually packaged products on sale at grocery stores. This is true of some cereal, diapers, bread, tuna, potato chips, milk, plastic bags, frozen foods, fresh meats, and paper products (when comparing paper products, don't forget to take the thickness into consideration—one- or two-ply, as well as the number of sheets per roll). Watch your local stores' bulk section. Many carry a section of bulk-packaged items just like a warehouse club. Many times the local store will charge the same or less than the warehouse club.

Knowing your prices is crucial. The packages are larger than we are used to, and it's harder to determine if it's a good deal. Some things are cheaper, but many things actually are more expensive than at regular grocery stores. Taking your price list along helps. Many people fall into the trap of thinking everything is less at a warehouse club than at a regular grocery store, so they buy whatever they need or want. This can be financially deadly. For example, one warehouse club sells their own brand of paper products at 2.5 times higher (that's 250 percent) than its equivalent at local stores. I also think the quality of these paper products is inferior to items I buy elsewhere for less. These higher prices are scattered throughout the store. A good example of this is name-brand over-the-counter drugs. On my last visit I compared the price of Bayer aspirin and found that the unit price of the jumbo size I would have to buy at the warehouse club cost more than at the local grocery store. You need a calculator and your price list for safe maneuvering.

When we compare items, we must remember that store-brand equivalents sell at a much lower price. Warehouse clubs mainly sell well-advertised name brands. This alone makes their prices higher on many items. A warehouse club will usually be cheaper if you only compare the name brands to their prices at a grocery store. But we must not forget the great alternatives found in generic and store brands. Occasionally a warehouse club will sell their own brand (beyond the paper products mentioned above). Many of these brands are equally as good as the name-brand equivalent. Some off brands are even the same item. Many companies buy items from the name-brand corporations and sell them under their own label. Stores make more profit when they sell their own brand. They have eliminated the middleman and can sell for less than any competitor and still make a good profit. The warehouse clubs know this and are beginning to add more of their own brands. The quality of most store-brand items is improving greatly. They know you won't settle for less, so they continually improve the flavors, textures, and durability of their goods.

Warehouse clubs should be a tool just like other resources. They should be used only for those things that cost less. When I stick to this plan, I stay within my budget. But I am as easily tempted as anyone. And warehouse clubs can be very tempting. I tend to overbuy foods when I shop at these stores. I buy more of some items than we normally need, and the food is consumed as quickly as when I buy less—even when we aren't hungry. If it's there, we eat it. I am tempted by the convenience foods that are cheaper than at grocery stores. But I must remind myself that making them at home is even cheaper—and healthier. And I must remind myself of my goal, my reason for making that choice.

I often am asked if joining a warehouse club is worth the cost. I believe the answer is yes. It is a fair question that each person needs to calculate. I don't like that I have to pay to shop at a store, but if I am careful about what I buy, I come out ahead every year.

If you watch your prices, and only buy those items that are good buys, it is worth it, and you will recoup your membership fee and more. Otherwise, if you buy everything your home needs at this type of store, you could be paying a membership fee in order to spend as much as you would at a regular grocery store.

Another factor to consider before deciding to shop at these types of stores is whether you can handle the temptations. If you are an impulse shopper, you will do better to shop elsewhere. The good deals are not worth it. The overwhelming nature of these stores can cause you to spend more than you would if you had shopped at a regular store.

To help you maneuver through the aisles of these warehouse stores, I have listed good buys and bad buys. I tried to pick commonly used items. This is by no means a complete list. It will merely help you to start your own research. Remember that each store's prices may vary and prices change weekly in some areas. The prices I quote here are as of January 2001 and may vary at your local stores.

$\mathcal{G}$OOD DEALS (a good sale price) AT A WAREHOUSE CLUB

- Off-brand over-the-counter drugs:
    acetaminophen and ibuprofen (1.5¢ per pill)
    pseudoephedrine (8¢ per pill)
    aspirin (3.8¢ per pill)
- Some personal care products:
    Colgate toothpaste (22¢ per oz./$1.69 per tube)
- Spices and gravy mixes (40¢ per serving)
- Batteries ($2 per 4-pack)
- Some paper products:
    paper towels (79¢ per roll)
- Most peanut butters (8.7¢ per oz.)
- Some cereals (8.3¢ per oz.)
- Cheese ($1.40–$1.53 per lb.)
- Butter ($1.59 per lb.)
- Milk ($2.10 per gal.) Beware of quality: may spoil quickly.
- Canned tuna (45¢ per 6 oz. can)
- Jams (8¢ per oz.)
- Pasta (43¢ per lb.)

- Eggs (79¢ per dozen)
- Flour (14¢ per lb.)
- Chocolate chips (7¢ per oz.)
- Office supplies (varies)

Some convenience items may be good buys at warehouse clubs. I didn't list these because they are items I don't buy.

*B*AD DEALS (can find on sale for less elsewhere) AT A WARE-HOUSE CLUB

- Name-brand over-the-counter drugs:
     Bayer Aspirin (6¢ per pill)
     Advil (3.5¢ per pill)
     Children's Tylenol (6.3¢ per pill)
- Household products:
     household cleaning products
     Cascade Gel (4¢ per oz.)
- Vegetable oil (store brand is cheaper)
- Light bulbs (36¢ per bulb)
- Plastic bags (store brand is cheaper)
- Some paper products:
     toilet paper (42¢ per roll)
     tissues (99¢ per box of 95)
- Most lunchmeats ($3 per lb.)
- Some boxed cereal (16¢ per oz. vs. 10¢ at regular store for same)
- Most salad dressings (10¢ per oz.)
- Sugar (38¢ per lb.)
- Frozen chicken ($2.10 per lb.)
- Fresh meat (varies)
- Frozen concentrated juices (89¢ per can)
- Bottled juices (varies)
- Candy (varies)

To compare these prices with my target prices, please read the Price Goals chart in chapter 5, "Keep Track of Food Prices."

Stretch the Season

$ $ $

*G*ardening is the number one hobby in America, but it is also a good way to cut grocery costs. I know friends who have converted one of the yards (back or front) of their home into a large vegetable garden. These friends grow their own produce and don't buy any fruits or vegetables all summer. One friend calculated the cost of each organic tomato she grew at 1¢ each. That's a great savings from the store-bought at 20¢–75¢ each.

If you don't have a large yard, plant a small garden. Many magazines have special editions on how to use a small space to produce vegetables. A four-by-eight-foot raised garden box can produce an abundant harvest. I use every space, including the fence where I grow berry vines. Don't limit yourself to the dirt on the ground. I have also used hanging pots to grow produce. I had a series of pots running around the eaves of my house in which I grew strawberries, carrots, cherry tomatoes, and herbs. If you have no yard at all, many cities offer a community plot. There are sometimes two to three lots per city. They give you a large plot of your own, all the water you need, and free mulch for a low annual fee (San Jose charged $60 per year). This comes to $5 per month. For fresh, organic produce, you can't spend less than that at a store.

For those who want to try a hand at converting their yard into a garden, here are some cost-saving tips.

- Fertilizer is free from horse stables and chicken farms.
- Mulch is free in some cities if they have a recycling program.
- Make your own compost in a small container. There are books at the library on how to do this.
- For bedding borders, collect rocks at a local creek.
- Seeds go on sale in March at most stores. Many avid gardeners, however, recommend ordering seeds from catalogs. They say the quality is better.
- Some types of seeds (not "hybrid" seeds) can be successfully harvested and replanted the following year. Be careful on storage—seeds don't like it too hot or too cold.

To decide which vegetable or fruit to grow, look at the amount of yard needed, the yield the item will give you, and the climate. For example, a zucchini plant takes up a very large area, but a tomato vine does not. But both require a hot climate and won't do well in cool areas. There are even hybrid plants that grow several vegetables and fruits together. Some smart farmers have grafted fruit tree limbs of several types to one trunk, allowing a good harvest out of limited space. I have even heard of tomato plants with potato plants grafted onto them so that above ground you get one type of vegetable and below ground you get another.

For a more thorough discussion on gardening, soil types, climates, and plant hardiness, please read the chapter on gardening in my book *Frugal Families—Making the Most of Your Hard-Earned Money*.

The main challenge of growing your own produce, or having friends who do, is the sudden surplus of one item. What do you do with thirty pounds of tomatoes all at once? One way to avoid this problem is to plant in shifts. Plant one row one week, another the next week, etc., so that they ripen in shifts as well. If you are the recipient of bushels of produce from generous friends, there are ways to stretch the produce to last all year. Remember that our farming ancestors learned this art. That's how they had food all year round. Preserving is done by salting, pickling, canning, freezing, and drying. I recommend these methods if you have an abundance of any food item. You won't need to buy that food again all year.

To preserve my bounty, I make a bunch of meals or snacks

from that one food item and then freeze them. For example, I'll make a ton of jam, zucchini bread, and tomato sauce. I then have what I need all year. Following are some tips I selected from my notes. They are mainly for excess zucchini, pumpkin, tomatoes, and fruits. I picked these produce items because they are the most commonly grown in home gardens.

ZUCCHINI

Tips

Zucchini can be frozen but will be mushy when thawed. I freeze them in the form I will use them when thawed. I grate them or slice them and store in meal-sized portions.

Uses

Other good uses for zucchini are zucchini pancakes, zucchini bread, zucchini relish, and spaghetti sauce with grated zucchini in it.

TOMATOES

Tips

- Select firm, tight-skinned tomatoes with deep color. They should feel heavy. "Light" feeling tomatoes are usually pulpy with little taste.
- Refrigerate only very ripe tomatoes, uncovered, no more than four days.
- If you have unripened tomatoes on the vine, but frost is imminent, pull up the whole vine and hang it upside down in a cool, dark place. They will ripen slowly over a few weeks.
- When cooking with fresh tomatoes, avoid aluminum, which can react with the acid in tomatoes to create an unpleasant taste.
- In cooked tomato dishes, a pinch of sugar helps the flavor.

Miserly MOMS

- Never wash a tomato until just before use. Washing increases the risk of spoilage.
- To peel a tomato, try these two easy ways: First, place the tomato in boiling water for thirty seconds, then place in cold water. The skins will pull right off. Another method adds flavor to the tomato. Place the tomato on the end of a fork and hold it over a gas flame, turning constantly, until the skin blisters. Pull the skin off with a paring knife.
- Freeze any tomatoes not needed. Freeze them whole and when fully ripened. When they thaw, the skin falls right off and the fruit has the texture of a stewed tomato.

Uses

Tomatoes can be sliced, then dried, for storage as well as for flavor. Make large batches of salsa, spaghetti sauce, or tomato soup.

Many enjoy picking tomatoes when they are green and frying them, a southern dish. To make fried green tomatoes, dip green tomato slices in flour or cornmeal. Fry in oil until golden. For the best flavor, fry in bacon drippings.

PUMPKIN

To cook a pumpkin, cut it in half and scrape out the seeds. Place the two halves (open side down) on a cookie sheet and bake in a slow oven (300°) until tender (20–40 minutes). Scrape out the pumpkin and discard the shells. Use the cooked pumpkin the same way as you would canned pumpkin.

Uses

Pumpkins have many uses. The flesh can be used to make pumpkin bread, pumpkin pancakes, pumpkin pie, pumpkin cheesecake, and pumpkin tomato soup. Pumpkin seeds are a favorite in our house. We toss oil and salt on them and bake until golden brown.

134

$\mathscr{F}$RUITS

Lemons

When I get bags of lemons from friends, I juice them all and freeze the juice in ice cube trays. Then I pop the cubes into plastic bags and keep them year round for whenever I need it for cooking or lemonade. One cube is the juice of about half a lemon.

Apples

When my mom's apple tree is in season, we suddenly have lots of great apples. We eat the best of them and store the rest by making applesauce (simply boil them down and mash with a fork), cobbler, apple butter, or freezing slices in plastic bags for pies or drying them (thinly slice and lay on baking sheet overnight at 200°).

Berries

Growing your own berries is the best way to enjoy these lovely fruits. When a berry is vine-ripened, it is much sweeter than any store-bought version. If you cannot grow your own, visit a local farm that allows you to pick your own fruit. When in California, we visited a berry farm forty miles away. Many questioned the cost savings when you factor in the gas consumed in driving. But the day was a fun outing for the whole family, and we enjoyed the fresh farm air together. The raspberries and strawberries we picked were priced 75 percent less than the store's price. We made jam and cobblers that lasted for months. Making jams are the best way to use up extra fruits before they spoil. Most cookbooks have recipes for making jams and jellies. Frozen fruit pops, fruit leather, and fruit juice are also great uses for extra fruit.

Cranberries

After Thanksgiving fresh cranberries go on sale. Buy several bags of these to make into juice or jelly. They can be frozen for up to one year.

Homemade cranberry sauce is preferred at our house over the canned variety. Make a bunch and freeze the extra. Who says cranberry sauce can only be used at Thanksgiving?

RESOURCES

The Complete Idiot's Guide to Gardening, Jane Connor and Emma Sweeney (Alpha Books, 1996).

Low-Cost Gardening, Ian Walls (Ward Lock, 1992).

Rodale's Complete Garden Problem-Solver: Instant Answers to the Most Common Gardening Questions, Cheryl Long (Rodale Press, 1998).

Rodale's Organic Gardening Solutions: Over 500 Answers to Real Life Questions From Backyard Gardeners, Cheryl Long (Rodale Press, 2000).

Stocking Up: How to Preserve the Foods You Grow, Naturally, Carol Stoner (Rodale Press, 1973).

Vegetables Step-by-Step, Rita Buchanan (Better Homes and Gardens Books, 1997).

CHAPTER EIGHTEEN

Dinner on Meeting Night

$ $ $

*T*he clock has struck five. You dash to your car and make your way to the freeway. You navigate the traffic. You hope your kids will be ready to jump into the car when you get there. All the while you are wondering if you will get the kids fed, make it to the meeting on time, and not get indigestion. Sound familiar? Anyone with a regular weeknight activity knows the scenario.

Too often the meal on these nights is from a fast-food restaurant. The convenience is nice, but the cost can add to your indigestion. A meal made at home costs an average of $3 to $5 for a family of four. A fast-food meal for four averages $15 to $20. Some quick math reveals that this weekly ritual can cost you an extra $60 per month.

Hopefully a home-cooked meal would be better than the weekly fast-food feast. Fresh vegetables (and not just potatoes), tasty entrees, healthier ingredients, and less fat, sodium, and preservatives are the benefits. These facts, added to the financial motivations, lead me to find a better way.

I have come up with two ways to tame the meeting-night frenzy. Both of these ways require cooking in advance. If the thought of cooking once per month sends shivers down your spine, don't give up yet. There is an easy way to cook in advance on a busy schedule.

My first suggestion is for those in a family who can gather at home for a few minutes before the meeting. On a previous night that does not have a meeting scheduled, double the recipe for that night's dinner. Store it in the refrigerator (no more than three days). Chop lettuce and carrots for a salad (this is a quick vegetable), and store them in separate bags.

On meeting night, all you have to do is heat the meal and toss the salad in a bowl. It will take the same amount of time as driving through the fast-food restaurant. And it will cost significantly less. This is also a great night to reheat leftovers, or CORD (clean-out-refrigerator day).

So what does the family do that can't gather at home before a meeting? On days like that, I pack a picnic dinner the night before. It can be the extra dinner from a doubled recipe earlier in the week, or something as simple as sandwiches, salad, fruit, and rolls or muffins. For drinks, I fill a thermos. All of this is packed the night before.

If you are going to be away from home most of the day of the meeting, take the meal with you. Put it in the refrigerator at your (or your spouse's) workplace. If that won't work, drop it at the meeting location earlier in the day during errands when you are nearby. Most churches and other such meeting places have refrigerators.

If neither of these are options for you, invest in a small cooler and freezer packs. There are even small refrigerators for the car that run off of the cigarette lighter. This may be the best choice for those really on the go.

You might say, "This can't be very miserly!" If the fast-food meals cost you $60 per month, how long will it take to pay for the cooler? Not long.

The key to surviving meeting night with your sanity and your wallet is to plan ahead. In our house it has saved us a great deal of money over the years. Even if I had the extra cash to go to fast-food restaurants every week, I would rather see it go to a good cause or another budget category than to a fast-food company.

CHAPTER NINETEEN

Birthdays, Holidays, and Special Occasions

$ $ $

*W*hen it's time for a special occasion, we tend to throw the budget out the window. We think things like "Oh, it's their birthday" or "But it's Christmas!" I think we try to make ourselves feel better about not being creative at times like these.

Should we be sending the message that love and money are related? I have found that what people really want are your efforts and thoughts toward them. A simple party and homemade gifts mean more than extravagance. I think the same goes for our kids. A room full of toys is overwhelming. A few well-chosen items are better received.

So how do I keep the gift and party madness from putting me in debt for months? First, I plan what we are going to spend. I list all of the people we usually buy gifts and/or cards for (birthdays and holidays) for the entire year, any expected graduation or wedding gifts, baby showers, and the parties we usually throw (birthday, Christmas, Thanksgiving, monthly church potluck, etc.). Then we decide the maximum amount we will spend on each person for each occasion. We then add up the year's total and divide by twelve. This gives us the amount we need to set aside each month in order to achieve those goals. If it's too much for our budget, we scale back on certain events or gift giving and stick to it.

Following are some ideas I have used for birthdays, Christmas gifts, and dates with my husband. I hope they help your household.

BIRTHDAYS

I keep birthday parties as simple as possible. A homemade cake, a few close friends, and a local city park usually are adequate. What kids enjoy most is playing with their friends and family. If more is desired, you can add simple games such as bubble wands, charades, homemade piñatas (paper-mache around a balloon), potato rolling with a spoon, or catching water balloons. You also can make the cake into an animal shape. There are several books on cake shape ideas at the library.

Another party idea is to sleep in the backyard in a tent with a few buddies. Or have a pizza party—where they make the pizzas. Or have a bubble party. Make a huge amount of bubble solution (ten cups water to one cup Dawn or Joy—other brands don't bubble as well). Fill a wading pool with this. Hand out Hula-Hoops, and have the children stand in the hoop and pull a bubble around them. Hand out coffee cans that have both ends removed: they dip the opening in bubbles and blow out a huge bubble. Have them make their own wands by shaping coat hangers into shapes. (Closely supervise this, since the ends are sharp.) Once the shape is completed, duct-tape the ends.

If you like to give gift bags to the guests, scale those down too. Buy colored lunch sacks and let the kids decorate them with stickers and markers. Buy bulk candy or bulk tiny toys at warehouse clubs or party supply stores. Don't pay several dollars for each child's bag just because that's what is available at local stores.

If you'd like to go on an outing for the party, such as to the local zoo, take the lunch and cake along. Buying food and cake from the party location will cost significantly more—as much as four times.

There are numerous books in the library on fun, inexpensive birthday party ideas. My favorite is *Birthday Parties for Children: How to Give Them, How to Survive Them* by Jean Marzollo. It is full of age-appropriate party and game ideas that anyone can pull off.

As my kids become teens, their tastes in parties have changed.

Sometimes teens don't want parties anymore. Some would prefer to go to the movies with one or two friends, or go miniature golfing. Mine prefer to go with one friend to an amusement park or a movie. I give them the budgeted amount I would have spent on a party. I usually am able to get discounted tickets to the park through organizations or stores that offer them at the beginning of each season. This leaves them enough money to buy food. Any extra purchases have to come from their own money.

There is no harm in limiting the size or expense of a birthday party. We don't get everything we want as adults. We shouldn't give our children the message that they can have whatever they want—especially if we can't afford it. That could inspire them to later use credit to satisfy their impulses.

When you give a gift to another child, try to apply your miserly ways. I am not cheap in what I give, but I plan and watch for good prices. If I wait until the invitation arrives, I will likely have to run to the store and pay full price for a toy. One creative idea that a friend does is to buy wooden baking tool sets (rolling pin, small board, knife) when they are on sale during the "dollar days" events at her local grocery store. She buys several for future parties. When the time comes, she makes homemade scented play dough (see chapter 29, "Crafts for Kids") and wraps it with the baking set. This gift costs her $2. Another idea is to stock up on small toys when they are on sale and store them until needed. Don't give cash. You'll give more than you would spend on a toy.

$\mathcal{H}$OLIDAYS

Holiday celebrations should be run in the same manner. The focus should be on the friends and relatives, not the food and gifts. To scale down the cost of entertaining, try to change the type of party. Instead of serving dinner, serve dessert or have "tea." Or have an hors d'oeuvre party with some inexpensive items. There are many good cookbooks at the library and Web sites that specialize in inexpensive hors d'oeuvre recipes. If you want to serve a dinner, make the main dish and let others bring the side dishes. Or make dishes with less meat in them, or meatless altogether (try a vegetarian lasagna, for example).

Table decorations can be homemade. Find a craft for the kids to make that will look nice on the table. They'll have fun, and the guests will enjoy seeing their artwork. Check out a book on napkin folding from the library. This free activity can make a beautiful table.

Gift ideas for adults can be tricky. But I still believe the same principle that applies to children's gifts applies to adult gifts. What people want is thought and effort, not money or expensive gifts. I try to make my gifts for friends and relatives. Here are a few of my favorite ideas:

- Make a sachet from a small piece of fabric with a simple ribbon tie. Fill it with any of the following: rose petals, cotton balls with vanilla powder, cinnamon sticks with orange peels and cloves, or lavender flowers.
- I enjoy baking or cooking gifts. Some of my favorites from the kitchen are Spiced Nuts and Orange-Chocolate Truffles.
- For Valentine's Day I make strawberry milk shakes with red food coloring and bake heart-shaped cookies, pancakes, or pizza.
- Save the seeds from your garden harvest and make simple paper seed packets for each seed type. Decorate the packets for a personal gift.
- Give a movie pass and a bag of special popcorn kernels.
- Give a layered mix in a jar.

These are just a few ideas for gift giving that I have compiled over the years. There will be an entire section of them in my forthcoming cookbook, *Miserly Meals*.

When a baked or homemade item is inappropriate, I buy something on sale. I shop in advance of the holiday and watch for sales. I try never to pay full price. Waiting to shop near the holiday will only cost more. Few things are on sale then, and you'll be tempted to pick items you wouldn't normally buy.

SPECIAL OCCASIONS AND DATES

My husband and I need some time alone (as do most couples). We like to go on dates but can't usually afford the combined cost of a sitter, dinner at a restaurant, and/or movie theater tickets. So we've come up with some cheaper alternatives that are as much fun. Try one to see how it works for you.

Inexpensive Date Ideas

- ♥ Go on a walk at sunset. It's beautiful and relaxing.
- ♥ Pick a handful of wild flowers for your partner.
- ♥ Go for a bike ride.
- ♥ Go rummage through a flea market.
- ♥ Visit a local art or natural history museum.
- ♥ Go to a local bookstore's readings of poetry—or just browse.
- ♥ Go stargazing. Many community colleges have free observatory nights.
- ♥ Go on a free tour near you (winery, factory, etc.).
- ♥ Take a picnic basket to a park (if it's rainy, do it indoors and pretend).
- ♥ Go out for coffee and dessert instead of dinner.
- ♥ Go to matinees vs. nighttime shows. (Check with your employer. Some sell theater tickets at half price.)
- ♥ Go miniature golfing.
- ♥ Use two-for-one coupons for restaurants.
- ♥ When it's too cold to walk outdoors, walk in a mall.
- ♥ Send the kids to someone's house for the night and enjoy the silence.
- ♥ Put the kids to bed early and enjoy a candlelight dinner—alone.

RESOURCES

Birthday Parties for Children: How to Give Them, How to Survive Them, Jean Marzollo (Galahad Books, 2000).

Cake Decorating Bible, Anness Publishing Staff (Anness Publishing, Ltd., 2000).

Family Fun Activity Book, Bob Keeshan (Deaconess Press, 1995).

Family Fun Parties: 100 Party Plans for Birthdays, Holidays, and Every Day, Deanne Cook (Hyperion, 1998).

Free Family Fun and Super Cheap, Cynthia MacGregor (Replica Books, 2001).

Holiday Theme Parties: Entertaining Ideas, Decorations, and Recipes for Nine Unique Parties, Creative Publishing Staff (Creative Publishing, 2000).

www.party411.com. A Web site filled with party themes, budget planners, checklists, food, suggested gifts, decorations, and more!

CHAPTER TWENTY

Baby Care

$ $ $

*A*fter sharing some tips on how to save money on baby necessities with my friend, she encouraged me to write a chapter on saving with babies. Here I cover all the expenses that caused a squeeze on our pocketbook when we had our babies.

*D*IAPERS

I won't revisit the old debate of cloth versus paper, but I will share my discoveries regarding the costs only. The debate over the environmental impact of disposable diapers versus the air and water pollution caused by diaper services is an interesting one if you choose to look into it.

After evaluating this issue, I compared the average cost of 100 newborn-sized diapers. The most expensive alternative was a diaper service. It costs twice the amount of off-brand disposable or do-it-yourself cloth diapers. And in my research I found that do-it-yourself cloth diapers cost almost the same as off-brand disposables. The difference was only $2 per month less for cloth diapers. The reason cloth diapers are not much cheaper is the high cost of the initial purchase plus the cost of the hot water wash and the hot dryer. This adds up to quite a bit per load, and most families do three to five diaper loads per week. Of course, utility costs vary everywhere, but an average hot water wash with a hot dryer costs about $1.25. If you do 3 to 5 loads per week, that comes to $15 to

$25 per month. That is not factoring in the initial purchase of the diapers. This is only a few dollars less per month than store-brand disposable diapers. And we never had leaking problems with the off-brands. Many are actually name-brand diapers that were relabeled by an off-brand company.

*B*ABY FOOD

Sometimes we believe we need the products from the store shelves to properly care for our babies. But this is not always true. And making your own baby food can save you $2000 a year!

I found that if I mixed food I had cooked for dinner (minus the spices) with a few teaspoons of liquid in the blender, the food would be as good as store-bought. This costs significantly less than a jar of pureed baby food—up to fifteen times less!

There are many types of grinders available to make the food fine enough for the baby. If you don't have one, you can use your blender with good results. You don't need a special appliance for this. For meat, I boiled the beef or chicken until well done, put it in a blender, and added a bit of water, formula, or milk to provide a smooth consistency. Do the same with boiled vegetables. Adding milk or formula will provide extra protein where needed. For fruit, boiling helps make it soft enough to blend well.

I found I did not want to be grinding food while trying to prepare a meal for the family. So I learned to make my baby food in large portions. I stored it by filling ice cube trays with the food. I made a batch of chicken and designated one tray for chicken. I made a tray of some type of vegetable, and another for fruit. I defrosted one square at a time, which was just the right size for a meal.

*T*HE EXPENSE OF FORMULA

Bottle-feeding with formula can be excessively expensive, adding up to $200 per month for one child. Formula can range in price, depending on whether it is powder, liquid, name brand, or hypoallergenic. But even when the cheapest type is purchased, the cost is still high.

Breastfeeding, on the other hand, is free. Even if a mother has to return to work after her maternity leave, pumping breast milk and storing it in the refrigerator to be used the next day is better on the pocketbook and the baby. I did this while I was still working after the birth of my first child.

Breastfeeding is the most cost-effective and healthy way to feed an infant. Studies have shown that the nutrients in breast milk are what babies need to develop their brains and bodies. Many researchers go a step further and show that formula is often unhealthy, being filled with corn syrup, hydrogenated oils, artificial flavorings, and even preservatives.

If a problem exists and the mother worries that her child isn't getting enough milk with breastfeeding, her doctor or her local La Leche League chapter (*www.lalecheleague.org*) can assure her that the child is growing well.

*B*ABY WIPES

By making these yourself, you can save a lot of money. I figure that a canister of homemade wipes costs forty cents. Aside from the container of wipes on the changing table, we carry a canister of them in the car for messy faces and fingers. I also refill my travel pack with them so I have some in my purse at all times. The recipe:

One roll of strong and thick paper toweling
    (I prefer Viva's ultra thick, 50-count)
2¼ C. water
2 T. baby shampoo (for sensitive skin use Mennen's
    Baby Bath)
1 T. baby oil
1 round plastic container, at least 6 inches high

Cut the roll of toweling in half (making 2 smaller rolls). Use a large cutting knife and sharpen it right before cutting and again during cutting. Do not use a serrated knife. Set aside one half of the roll for another day. Remove the cardboard tube by grabbing the edge of it with a pair of pliers and twisting as you pull. If the roll you have is too large for your container, pull some of the paper out with the tube so that it will compress to fit. Combine the wet ingredients in the container (before placing the toweling in), and set aside one cup of the mixture. Place the roll in the container (you may need to squeeze it a bit to fit). Pour the cup of liquid on top of the paper to saturate. Pull the wipes from the center of the roll.

*B*ABY-SITTING

The cost of baby-sitting can make going out a rare occasion. If a few moms form a baby-sitting co-op, everyone benefits. Most co-ops trade one-hour coupons instead of money for watching each other's kids. Each club varies on how they handle multiple children. Most common is to charge an extra coupon per hour, per child. To start one, ask your friends and neighbors if they are interested. It only takes a few moms to get one started. Make coupons for one-hour sitting and start each member with a pack of ten (or whatever your group decides). Have a questionnaire for each member with basic questions: when is she not available; how does she feel about colds; does the family have pets, a pool, firearms, or other potential threats to a child's safety; is she willing to do overnights. These forms can then be copied for each member, allowing each mom to pick whomever she prefers to do the sitting.

*T*OYS

The cost of toys can be high. We try to keep the cost down by shopping good quality resale shops. We also shop the sales at toy stores. Each store has a clearance bin with some treasures in it. We have found $25 games for $7. For a special item, we save and look for it on sale.

When the holidays are over and the New Year's Eve dishes are still sitting in the sink, your checkbook is probably in shock. The last thing you probably want to think about is more toys. But that is actually the best time to think about it. Toys and gifts are going to be on sale. Many stores want to clear out the excess inventory left after the holidays. Buy that birthday gift for the kids that they didn't get for Christmas. Some of the best deals come from the warehouse clubs clearing out their excess toys.

If there is no conceivable way you can buy any more right now, don't panic. Many items go on sale a few times throughout the year. These are great times to buy for birthdays or even for the next Christmas.

When junior loses an important part of a toy, we tend to buy the whole toy to replace it. To save money, and toys, try contacting the manufacturer for that lost or broken piece. Most companies are very helpful and understanding. Here is a list of some of the major manufacturers to help you save your toys:

Fisher-Price. . . . . (800)–432–5437
Lego Systems . . . . (800)–422–5346
Little Tykes. . . . . (800)–321–0183
Brio. . . . . (800)–558–6863
Hasbro . . . . (800)–242–7276*
Playskool. . . . . (800)–752–9755*
Milton Bradley . . . . (413)–525–6411*

Toy Containers

I was getting tired of all those little toys scattered on the floor or sitting in a pile in the kids' rooms. So I began reusing many of our containers as storage bins for those little things. I use oatmeal boxes, large yogurt containers, large plastic containers that bulk pretzels come in, and boxes. No need to buy that expensive container box that the toy manufacturer wants you to believe you need.

RESOURCES

Baby Bargains: Secrets to Saving 20 Percent to 50 Percent on Baby Furniture, Equipment, Clothes, Toys, Maternity Wear, and Much, Much More!, Denise and Alan Fields (Windsor Peak Press, 1999).
Bargains-by-Mail for Baby and You, Dawn Hardy (Prima Publishing, 1992).
Products Basics: The Busy Person's Guide to Baby Products on a Budget, Renee M. Rolle-Whatley (Sandcastle Publishing, 1991).

*These companies have order forms for parts at: *www.hasbro.com/consumer/forms.htm.*

So That's What They're For! Breastfeeding Basics, Janet Tamaro (Adams Media Corp., 1998).

Super Baby Food, Ruth Yaron (F. J. Roberts Publishing, 1998).

The Womanly Art of Breastfeeding, Gwen Gotsch and Judy Torgus (Plume, 1997).

CHAPTER TWENTY-ONE

The Cost of Working

$ $ $

*W*orking is very expensive. This may seem confusing to some, since most of us were raised to believe that if your expenses go up so must your income in order to compensate. Losing half of our income, however, helped us realize that there were many hidden costs in working.

When I chose to stay at home with my children, we assumed we would have to move to a less expensive suburb to compensate for the 50 percent loss of income. But when I couldn't go through with the move, we were in a pickle: same house, same lifestyle, half the money. Even though I wanted to be at home full time, I looked at working part time out of desperation. Soon I realized how much working had cost me. Many expenses had surprisingly disappeared after I quit.

Financial experts have calculated the cost of working at anywhere from $9 to $25 per hour. I was stunned when I learned this! That meant that if I took a job paying $10 per hour, I might only see $1 for every hour I worked.

Here are some of the expenses that went into these experts' calculations:

- child care
- taxes (local, federal, state)
- commuting fees (tolls, parking, etc.)
- gasoline and mileage

- car insurance (extra car, nicer car for the job, higher mileage, etc.)
- clothes (new clothes, cleaners, accessories, etc.)
- gifts for co-workers
- fast-food lunches and breakfasts out
- convenience foods at home
- extra eating out
- occasional housekeeping help
- hair care (professional looking cuts and styles)

Every person has a different cost of working. Some people have several children in day care, while others have no children. Some commute by car many miles to work, others ride a bike. Some can wear casual clothes to work, while others are required to dress in suits. Some pay more taxes than others. Use the list above to factor your cost of working.

After looking at my own experience, I soon realized that the experts' figures were accurate for me. I was spending $9 to $10 per hour for the privilege of working. My cost of working was $915 per month, or $10,980 per year.

When I stopped working, I spent less on clothes. Working sometimes requires special clothes. If not special ones, you need more outfits to rotate in your wardrobe than you do if you're at home. Few people wear the same five outfits to work in rotation each week. We tire of something long before it is not useful. So back to the department store we go. Then there is the cost of the accessories. For women, the cost of pantyhose alone is steep. And don't forget the shoes that need to match the outfits. And then there is the jewelry and other accessories. For men, the cost of suits or dress slacks is high. I discuss ways to reduce clothing expenses in chapter 22, "Clothing."

Aside from clothes, there is the cost of transportation and parking. Some need a nicer car than they would if they were not working: one they can use for the transport of clients or co-workers. Some families might be able to eliminate one car if someone didn't work. The cost of wear on the car and tires, plus gasoline, comes to 35¢ per mile (at the time of this writing). That's considerable when you see how many commuting miles you put on the car each day. Then there are the parking fees and added insurance for an extra car. In our area, they charge more if the car is used for commuting.

And then there is child care. The cost of child care can run from $350 to $900 per month per child. That's a lot of money. But I paid the money while I worked because I wanted the best for my child. Yet, though the care was excellent, I still wanted to be with my child and see how he was doing. Perhaps we should add to the experts' list of expenses the cost of counseling from all of the worrying we do about our kids and the stress we encounter by working. After three and a half years, I didn't want to do it anymore.

We must not forget the portion due to Uncle Sam when we work. And remember that the more we earn, the more he takes. Most two-income families have a higher tax bracket than a single-income family. If one parent stops working, the tax deductions from the other spouse's salary may fall into a lower tax bracket. This can add up to a substantial amount of money. The point where it can make a difference is currently around $42,000 (joint income). Please consult a tax advisor to verify this for your family.

We must not overlook the savings we can achieve on the purchases we need to make. I am speaking of gifts for co-workers, relatives, household items, appliances, and even furniture. When we are working, we can't scour the sales and look for the best deals. We can't slowly acquire our Christmas and birthday gifts year round as we see a sale somewhere. I'm not saying that working folks don't shop around or look for good deals. I am saying that they may be less able to watch for sales or visit several stores before making their purchases. When I was working, I sometimes had to "settle" for what seemed like a good deal because I had no time to go to several other stores to compare. Many people who work do make time for all of this shopping around, and they should be congratulated for their efforts. But they might be paying a higher price somewhere else, such as a lack of time with family members or hiring household help because their free time is spent elsewhere.

Another cost that many overlook is the additional food expense that working people incur. Working parents are very busy and very tired. They often forget or they don't want to make homemade lunches for themselves, so they eat out. Even if it's a cheap meal, it will run $4 to $6. Most of us work twenty days per month, so lunches could cost you $180 per month. Then there's dinner to prepare when you get home. The working parent often relies on convenience meals or eating out because they don't want to cook from scratch, or there isn't enough time to wait for the food to cook. These conveniences cost up to six times more than a homemade meal. While we were both working (even part time for me), our food bill was four times higher.

Once I looked at these expenses that vanished when I quit, I decided to total them. Then I combined these savings with the ways I was going to further reduce our spending (now that I had the time) to see the overall savings of not working.

Here is a list of the categories in which we further reduced our spending:

Category	Reduced By
Groceries	$250 per month
Not eating out	$125 per month
Clothes	$75 per month
Haircuts	$60 per month
Automobile (Gasoline & Insurance)	$50 per month
Medical insurance	$25 per month
Cleaning supplies	$10 per month
Total reduced spending	$595 per month

This amount combined with the loss of the "cost of working" makes for a healthy reduction in expenses.

Total reduced spending (from above)	$595 per month
My cost of working	$915 per month
Total saved by not working	$1,510 per month

$1,510 per month = $18,120 per year!

What this figure means to me is that if I returned to work, even part time, I would lose the first $18,000 of that salary to added expenses.

Many people are concerned that the time it takes to be thrifty doesn't make it worthwhile. This is not true. I figure that it takes me seven hours of thrifty work per week to make up what I was earning at my job.

Here is a breakdown of how that time is spent:

Hours Per Week to Be Miserly

Task	Time
Shopping	2½ hours
Planning	½ hour
Shopping extra stores (bread store, warehouse clubs, super sale somewhere)	¾ hour
Extra cooking (homemade versions of muffins, cookies, syrup, granola, relishes, snacks, etc.)	3 hours
Total	7 hours per week

CHAPTER TWENTY-TWO

Clothing

$ $ $

I spend about $500 per year on clothes for a family of four. The average American family spends more than $1,000 per year. Our clothes look nice, without stains and tears. In order to spend this little, we must plan what our clothing needs will be and shop carefully. I figure how many outfits, dresses, men's slacks, etc., we need each month or two. I then look for the best prices on these items. If I shopped at department stores without preplanning, I would probably spend $100 every time.

My annual total includes dress slacks for my husband, but not suits. When I buy slacks for him, I try to avoid those that require dry cleaning, as this expense adds up quickly. If suits are required for your husband's job, watch for sales at department stores and purchase two pairs of slacks for each jacket, since those are what wear out fastest. Buy neutral-colored pants and/or jackets so as to match future purchases.

If buying new clothes is a hardship, but you want your children to look nice, these are some good alternatives: I have found many great bargains at the "rerun" stores throughout our area. There are the big-name places such as Savers, Salvation Army, or Goodwill. Then there are the independent thrift stores in each city. Some of the wealthier neighborhoods might have a better selection of clothing to offer. Finding clothes may take some time, as the items come and go weekly.

There are also the seasonal resale stores (in our area there is one called Outrageous Outgrown) where a few well-organized women set up a store for a few days through which we can each sell our clothes, toys, etc., at prices we choose. Another idea that has helped many families here is to organize a clothing exchange. On a designated weekend, people bring in their used clothing and then take what they need from the selection. One day is for dropping off and the other is for "shopping." It's a great way to help each other out and to go home with newfound treasures. Ask your church or local community center to sponsor it. Each of these offers some great clothes at great prices.

If you prefer to buy new clothes, the best way is to watch sale flyers and stock up when prices are very low. One friend taught me to save even more by buying clothes one size too large for the children, and then loosely sewing the sleeve of a shirt into the cuff or a blouse sleeve into the shoulder seam and hemming the pants or skirts. When the kids grow, simply let out these allowances.

Garage sales and local flea markets have a lot of variety. When you see one with children's clothes and toys, stop and investigate. Again, the wealthier the neighborhood, the better the selection of items. I have found nice sweaters for a dime and good toys for one-tenth their value.

Buy used clothing at consignment shops or used clothing stores that offer top-quality brand-name clothing. No clothes are accepted that are worn or stained. You can save 50 percent off what you'd pay for retail.

Watch for sales at the discount clothing stores such as Ross, Dress for Less, or Marshalls. Many stores clear out fashions or seasonal clothes at 40 to 50 percent off. Stock up. One friend bought an excellent tie for $0.99 at Ross. Ties and/or dress shirts that are offered at a department store for $30 to $45 often can be found at discount stores for $5 to $15, and the brand names are the same. Adults shouldn't be growing anymore, so you can buy for next year with confidence that the clothes will fit. Check out their prices on socks and other accessories. They might be on sale as well.

Avoid the so-called sales at the big-name department stores. The bigger-name stores have inflated prices and then have 40 to

50 percent off "sales" to lure you in. Compare their prices to the discount department stores.

RESOURCES

Cash for Your Used Clothing, William R. Lewis (Client Valuation Services, 2000).

Secondhand Chic: Finding Fabulous Fashion at Consignment, Vintage, and Thrift Stores, Christa Weil (Pocket Books, 1999).

CHAPTER TWENTY-THREE

Help for the Working Mom

$ $ $

*I*n preaching the value of not working outside your home, I don't want to overlook the working mom. Many women truly must work, and perhaps you are one of them. You may have squeezed every penny you can from the budget, but it still isn't enough. Maybe you have had an unexpected emergency or another high expense your budget cannot absorb. You might be a single-income parent. Or perhaps you do not have any children and enjoy working, but you need help with your budget. Whatever the reason, this chapter is dedicated to helping the working womam stretch her dollar.

As I discussed earlier, the expense with the largest opportunity for savings is groceries. This is also true for working moms. After reviewing the eleven guidelines, I have summarized how working moms can apply them and make the best use of their limited time.

GROCERIES

You can still put a major dent in your food bill, but you will need to approach shopping and cooking differently. Most of the eleven guidelines can apply to the working mom, but the following are the best use of her time.

1. Plan your menus around the sale flyers

I cannot stress this point enough. This one step alone can cut your grocery bill by 30 percent. If you only have time for one trip to the store, make it work for you. Don't just drop in and buy what you need. Plan around the store's sales. Use their loss leaders as your basis for all meals, snacks, and produce.

2. Stock up on sale items

When your local store mails out a coupon book, use it. Go there only once each month and buy those things you generally use. Don't let low prices tempt you into buying things you wouldn't normally buy. Stock up on the things you regularly use and buy enough to last you six weeks. That's when another coupon book will come out.

3. Avoid convenience foods

It's so easy to depend on prepackaged foods, mixes, and frozen meals when you are busy working. But you pay for that ease. Most of those items cost four to six times more than a homemade version of the same thing. To make the most of your time, find the things you are paying the most for and replace them with homemade. If these are snacks and lunch box items, then make alternatives for those.

4. Avoid eating out

Make your own sack lunch. Those cafeteria and fast-food lunches add up. Avoid the vending machines, even for a soft drink. They charge three times more than you need to pay. Take a thermos of juice or a six-pack of soda and leave it in the office refrigerator. Don't grab coffee or breakfast at a restaurant or cafeteria on the way to work. Fill the coffeemaker the night before and flip the switch on your way to the shower in the morning. Grab a banana and toast if you're late. You'll save!

5. Do your shopping and cooking once a month

If you are working you may not have the time to go to three or more stores per week to get foods at the lowest prices. If you can't take full advantage of the loss leaders at several local stores, buying in bulk is your next best option. Shop the good deals when you can, buying enough for the month's meals. For example, buy chicken when it's on sale. And buy enough for the month.

With all this bulk food, you should then set aside one or two days per month to cook—part of a weekend works well. Prepare the month's meals and freeze them. Some people shop throughout the month for sales, then cook on a Friday night and a Saturday morning.

With this plan you will save money and time by:

- bulk buying (lower costs)
- homemade "convenience" meals in the freezer (reduces eating out)
- less time each evening spent cooking and washing pots and pans

CLOTHES

To combat the high cost of a work wardrobe, you must look at the styles you wear, where you buy them, and how you clean them.

As for the styles you wear, avoid trendy fashions. Don't buy anything that can only be worn alone, such as a fancy shirt or patterned dress. Stick with classic designs and colors that can be mixed and matched and that will still be in style five years from now. I buy neutral-colored shirts that can be worn with any neutral skirt or slacks. They can be combined with other neutral jackets or skirts for a completely different outfit. If I spent the same amount on a dress, I could only wear it once in a while, as opposed to the several times with the mix-and-match approach. The same goes for shoes. Don't buy red shoes for the red dress. You can only wear them with that outfit. Buy neutral colors (brown, tan, navy, gray, black) and wear them with all the outfits. Remember, you aren't running for fashion queen. You're trying to keep your money for your family.

Pick fabrics that can be hand- or machine-washed. The dry cleaners take a big chunk out of your budget. Buy lighter weight fabrics that can be worn in layers when it's colder, and alone when warm.

For underwear and pantyhose, buy in bulk from the manufacturers. Many have outlet stores in the malls. Most offer catalogs. Many have frequent-shopper cards that let you earn free purchases after a certain amount is spent. Buy their irregular or imperfect pairs to save even more. I have saved another 50 percent by buying irregulars. These have minor flaws, usually in the panty area. I have never had problems with them. Wash pantyhose by hand and rinse in fabric softener to help them last longer.

RESOURCES

The Complete Financial Guide for Single Parents, Larry Burkett (Victor Press, 1992).

The Working Mom's Book of Hints, Tips, and Everyday Wisdom, Louise Lague (Peterson's, 1995).

The Husband

$ $ $

*W*hen talking with a few friends about their budgets, one had a great question. How do you get your husband committed? That doesn't mean committed to an asylum, but committed to a budget and your miserly ways.

This may prove to be one of the harder parts of the miserly lifestyle. If you are pinching the copper from every penny but your husband eats out for lunch every day, you have a hole in the budget bag.

After the birth of our second child, I was too tired to shop. I sent my dear husband to the store with a list. He was not interested in my method of shopping at a few stores and only buying sale items. He went to one store and bought everything. He spent twice what we usually did for one week of groceries (the salsa and chips helped). I realized then that he needed to be convinced of the payoff in my method of shopping and the importance of my goal.

In order to get my husband to agree to the other spending changes I wanted to try, I needed to convince him that those changes would be easy and profitable. Men tend to want to see numbers on paper to help them understand. Many men think all you're doing is saving a few cents here and there. As you know, it's much more than that.

The best thing I did to convince my husband was to annualize the savings we could achieve. By reducing expenses and applying my guidelines to our groceries, I showed him I could save $7,140 per year from our current budget. By quitting my job, I could reduce other hidden expenses by another $10,980 per year. By doing both (quitting and applying miserly ways), I was saving our family more than $18,000 per year. I asked him what he could do with an extra $18,000.

The other thing that impressed my husband was the first major purchase made with the savings I had accumulated. After two months of miserly shopping and cooking, I had set aside enough money to buy six oak dining room chairs. That spoke to him.

Another thing that helped convince him this was all well worth the trouble was when I explained that it doesn't take that much time. It takes about seven hours per week to apply the things I have learned.

If all else fails, try to make a deal with him. Ask him how much he thinks he needs to spend each week (lunches, magazines, etc.). Then ask him if he would take that amount in cash and leave the rest to you. Then you can be a thrifty person in shopping, cooking, and other household expenses and show him how much you saved (cash speaks loudest) at the end of two to three months. If he enjoys eating lunch out, ask him if he'd take a sack lunch to work instead. Show him how much his lunches out are costing the family. Promise him you will make his lunch a tasty meal.

Another agreement that stops major leaks in a budget is that neither of you will buy anything over $5 without consulting your spouse. Before you drop your coffee cup, think about this idea for a moment. This policy doesn't apply to any "mad" money you each get as an allowance. You can spend that where you like without anyone's opinion. It's those trips to the department stores or the mall that get us into spending trouble. It's that cute outfit in the catalog, or a nice kid selling stuff to raise money for school. By having to discuss it, it gives you time to reflect on whether you really need it and to compare the price to somewhere else. It also curbs the impulse buying manufacturers hope we will succumb to.

Many husbands (like us wives) tend to have certain weak spots where they spend freely. My husband's weak spot was books. He could drop $100 a month in books. He justifies it because they were reference or research books and not junk. I needed to help him find an alternative way to satisfy this urge, or our financial ship was going to sink. We learned how the inter-library loan system worked. Your library can access almost any library in the U.S. We were amazed that you can check out any book you need with a free card. Even if the book is new, you can request it be purchased or borrowed from a library that just purchased it. We also discovered we could rent movies, CDs, and cassette tapes for free. This helped plug that hole in the ship. Be creative with any trouble spots your family has with money.

If all of these ideas still sound nuts, try writing down everything you spend for one month. Writing checks for everything helps in this endeavor. Then categorize what you spent (entertainment, food, subscriptions, clothes, household, hobbies, bank fees for overdraft charges, etc.) and figure the total for each category. See how much was wasted on trivia. Show your husband the damage. Also ask him how important it is to him to have his children raised by strangers at a day care, or by his wife for a few sacrifices. He might become a convert.

CHAPTER TWENTY-FIVE

Ten Ways to Get Kids to Save

$ $ $

*W*hile shopping, it is very easy to give in to a child's persistent whining about a toy or special treat, especially when you are holding a screaming baby, a toddler, a shopping list, and a diaper bag. It's easier to grab what is convenient or familiar and get out of the store as fast as possible.

These are the times when your miserly skills are tested severely. The best way to solve this weekly battle is to get your kids on your side. Help them to see the finances your way. Then you can reinforce what you've explained while shopping. Let me clarify. If junior understands there is a limited amount of money to be spent at the store, then he will say, "Oh yeah" when you remind him you can't afford that impulse item or more expensive brand of cereal.

It's hard to get them to understand that there is a limit to the green stuff when they see the cash machines spitting it out whenever we punch some buttons. My kids used to say, "What do you mean we don't have any more money? Just go to the bank machine or write a check."

Here are some tips that have helped my kids become involved:

1. Shop alone as often as possible

This, of course, is the ideal situation. You can compare prices as you need to and stop whenever you want to, regardless of what toys are in front of you (why do you think those toys are placed at their eye level?). And, most important, you can think. But reality is something different. During school hours there may be fewer kids in your shopping cart. Try shopping then.

2. Explain that you have a limited amount of money and choices have to be made

Explain the concept of a budget, and that plans have been made for all the money the family has. Use a pie chart with colors for each budget category. Exact numbers are not necessary to get the point across. Even five-year-olds can understand that there are basic limits.

3. While at a store, explain what amount you plan to spend at this particular store

If they are used to seeing you buy whatever you want when you go shopping, then they won't understand why they can't do the same. Let them see you put some things back when you realize you are spending beyond your budget.

4. Give them the facts: "I can't afford it"

Who says they should have everything they want? They are never too young to learn this principle.

5. Ask them if they want to use their allowance to buy it

When faced with the decision of whether or not to spend their own money, they quickly realize its value.

6. Use the opportunity to help them learn to make choices

Explain that if you buy a brand of cereal with the fancy toy inside instead of the generic one, the difference will prevent you from doing something else (a movie rental, or an outing of the same value) or buying some other food they want. Let them make the choice and then hold them to it.

7. For the very persistent (and young), let them pick one item that isn't budgeted

Give them a small amount of money ($1 to $2) that they can spend. This will keep them busy while you shop: they will switch and trade, keeping out of your way. All other wants have to be traded for that one, so that when you get to the cash register, their purchase is no more than their given amount.

8. When you are away from the store, let them see or learn about other economic lifestyles

Let them see you donate some of your income to help others. Explain how you planned for that donation in the budget. Take them with you to a homeless shelter or rescue mission to help serve food. Help them to learn about other cultures and our abundance.

9. If there is a certain item they always ask for, show them how the system works

Let them watch for sales and coupons in the grocery store fly-ers and Sunday coupons. My son loves a certain brand of ice cream that is very expensive. I normally don't buy ice cream un-less it's a great sale or I have a wonderful coupon. One day I found him on the floor going through the Sunday newspaper cou-pons. He found a great coupon for that brand of ice cream. He also saw that it was on sale at a local store. Eureka! At last he un-derstands! (And he got the ice cream.)

10. For those larger-ticket items, I have found two ways to tame them

First, I tell them to add the item to their Christmas or birthday list. I explain that most relatives enjoy getting a special item for them on a special occasion.

If they can't wait that long, I have them save their allowance for big-ticket items. If it's very expensive and special, I might match what they save.

Making a list of jobs for money around the home is also an incentive to earn the item faster. If they aren't interested in working for the item, then it must not be that important to them.

From these suggestions, I hope to teach my kids the value of money and of patience. We will be constantly challenged. It's worth it to stick to your guns during those hard times. They need to learn that love should not be measured by money.

How to Save with Teenagers

Someone said that my grocery spending goal was nice, but I must not have any teenagers in the house. She was right. I didn't have teenagers in the house when I first wrote this book. But I do now! And we are able to keep our food bill down to our goals. I have several friends who have teenagers who still keep their food bill down to $40 per week. The only way that is possible is to cook from scratch, avoid those convenient snack foods, and cook in bulk. Aside from those tips, here are a few others that pertain to saving with teenagers.

Food

- Watch the snacks! Snack foods and teenagers can be a costly combination. Make snacks once per month and keep on hand: cookies, muffins, breads, pizza, drinks, etc.
- If you can't make something very well (such as potato chips), stock up when they go on sale.
- Ask teens to use some of their own money for those non-essential snack foods.

Name-Brand Clothes

- Give them their allotted clothes money that would pay for good off-brand clothes on sale.
- Let them make up the difference for name-brand clothes by using their allowance and job money.
- Show them how to shop for their name-brand items at good resale, consignment, and thrift shops.

- Start assigning certain expenses to them (clothes, gas, cosmetics, entertainment, etc.)

It's better for teens to learn how to budget and experience mistakes while at home than to get into debt after they move out on their own.

RESOURCES

Money-Smart Kids, Janet Bodnar (Kiplinger Books, 1993).

Raising Money-Smart Kids—How to Teach Your Children the Secrets of Earning, Saving, Investing, and Spending Wisely, Ron and Judy Blue (Thomas Nelson Publishers, 1992).

The Totally Awesome Money Book for Kids and Their Parents, Adriane G. Berg (Prentice-Hall, 1993).

CHAPTER TWENTY-SIX

Miscellaneous Tips

$ $ $

*H*ere are some tips on various topics that didn't fit into other chapters. They may be small matters, but they add up. Most have to do with daily life, which, as we know, is where our money goes.

PHOTO-DEVELOPING SERVICES

If you haven't looked, there can be a significant difference in the prices of photo developing and printing. Prices can range from $3 to $20 for a 35mm roll of film.

Some people think that the more expensive service produces the best picture quality. I wish this were true. But the higher rates usually pay for fast service or a fancy name. The processing machines used by most developing houses are similar. Many stores send their film out to a central service. So it could be the same developer whether you drop the film off at a warehouse club, your local camera shop, or at Safeway. The fascinating thing I learned is that many of these central houses are available to us directly. Two of these are very accessible and reasonable—York and Clark.

A consumer magazine did a survey of the most frequently used film-developing companies, evaluating price, service, and quality. The best in all three categories were York and Clark. They charge very little for a roll of 35mm film, 24 exposures. I have used these services and was pleased. I get the pictures back in about a week. I can ask for faster service if I want to pay a small fee. Many customers complain about their service, instead of praise it. Most complaints fall into common categories: lost film, overexposed pictures, scratched negatives, or someone else's pictures in your envelope. Many of these problems can be avoided by taking some simple steps before you mail your film. And most of the problems could happen at a local photo lab just as easily as at the mail-order places—both are run by humans, and humans make mistakes.

To avoid lost film or receiving someone else's film, put a mailing label around each canister of film and only put one canister in each envelope. The envelopes sometimes break in the post office or at the lab, and the canisters fall out. Having your name and address on it can save it. Knowing what was on the film can sometimes help locate it, as they have some rolls that are developed but not claimed. They can look through these for you. I once had an envelope open at the post office. It would have been lost, but someone found my canister with my address label stuck around it and mailed it to me.

If your pictures arrive looking washed out, it may not be the lab's fault. You may have used the wrong speed of film for the lighting. Make sure you use the appropriate ASA (film speed) for your lighting. Other ways to make sure the pictures look good are to avoid putting your film in your luggage when flying. The X-ray machines in the baggage area are high-powered and can cause the film to be damaged. Carry it on board the plane and have them hand inspect the canisters and camera.

Scratched negatives are something that any film operator at any discount lab can cause. Even your local drugstore's film processing can cause scratches. The machines are the same, and operator error causes the scratches. Sending them to a mail-order lab runs no more or less risk of this happening.

Mail-order companies frequently send out mailers with a low introductory price. If you have not received one of their mailers, write to them at:

Clark Color Labs
Box 96300
Washington, D.C. 20090
www.clarkcolor.com

York Photo Labs
400 Rayon Dr.
Parkersburg, WV 26101
www.yorkphoto.com

Another place to get a similar price for film developing is through a warehouse club. They charge about the same as the mail-order companies and can get the pictures back faster than mail order. If you are already a member of a warehouse club, it may be worthwhile to have your film developed there. But if it will cause you to visit them more often and buy items you normally wouldn't buy, it would be cheaper in the long run to use mail-order developing.

GAS/CAR MAINTENANCE

Prices vary from station to station and region to region. I hear about people who drive across town to save five cents per gallon. That's only going to save $1 on a twenty-gallon fill-up. This doesn't warrant driving across town. But it is worth keeping in mind when you are in that part of town. There are usually certain stations that offer a lower price most of the time. Fill up when you are near them. To find the cheapest gas prices near you, visit *www.gaspricewatch.com.*

Some states still offer cheaper gas at cash-only stations. I have found some cash-only stations that regularly charge fifteen cents per gallon less than other stations. They are able to charge less because they don't have the overhead expenses of handling credit cards. Some cash-only stations have a reputation for poor quality gas, but this is not true of all. If your state offers this type of station, try filling up there. It can save $3 per fill-up or $12 per month with an average fill-up of once per week.

Another way to stretch your gas money is to fill up early in the morning when the air is still cool. The gas in the station's tanks expands as the heat of the day increases. So a fill-up in the afternoon will give you less gas (up to one gallon's worth) than a fill-up in the morning. It's important to not top off your tank, as the gas will expand as the day warms.

Here are some other ways to save on your gas expenses:

- With frequent oil changes, tune-ups, and checking the air in the tires, you can save an additional 15 percent on mileage.
- If you have a pickup truck, you can save 20 percent on your mileage by covering the bed. The wind causes a drag as it

scoops against the tailgate. The same is true of open sunroofs.

- Get the extra weight out of your trunk. It can also reduce your gas mileage.
- Watch your speed. A ten-mile-per-hour increase in speed on the freeway (65 versus 55 miles per hour) can reduce mileage by 17 percent.
- Turn off the engine if it will idle for more than one minute.
- Choose radial tires—these use 2 to 3 percent less fuel than other types.
- Turn off the air conditioning; it reduces gas mileage too.

Milk

There are a few ways to cut down on the cost of milk. If your household drinks a lot of the moo-juice, consider one of the following ideas.

The cheapest way to buy milk is to use instant milk. The nonfat dry milk runs about $2 per gallon as opposed to $3.59 per gallon of fresh milk. Most families can adapt and enjoy the savings (hint: the colder the mixed milk, the better it tastes). The nutrition is the same, and the lack of fat is a plus.

Some families buy whole milk and then water it down. This makes the milk taste similar to one percent extra-light milk and can reduce the cost of a gallon of milk by half. Other families combine both ideas. Mix equal parts of fresh milk with prepared powdered milk. The protein, calcium, and vitamins are the same, but the fat content is less and so is the cost. Another idea is to use the instant milk for baking. This can save one to two gallons of milk per week for some families.

If you live anywhere near a dairy, or see a great sale on milk, make the trip occasionally and stock up. You can freeze milk. The fat may separate after thawing, so shake it well before serving.

Bread Machines

Did you buy a bread machine because you thought it would be cheaper in the long run? Well, you might be wrong. I have thought long and hard about the value of a bread machine. I owned one for three years and then it broke. I wanted another one but couldn't afford the price tag. So I researched the savings one would bring. I found that for most homes, bread machines do not yield a savings.

I compared the cost of a store-bought loaf of plain white, whole wheat, and buttermilk bread with an equivalent loaf baked in a bread machine. The cost was about the same. Only multigrain bread was more expensive when purchased at a store than home-made in a bread machine.

If the multigrain loaf contained several types of grains (oats, wheat, wheat berries, sunflower seeds, sesame seeds, etc.), a store-bought multigrain loaf of comparable size would cost about $3.50 (if not on sale). A homemade loaf of equal size and grain usage would cost about $1.50.

I usually don't recommend buying a bread machine because most people don't use it much, or they intend to bake healthy whole-grain bread but usually make easy white bread instead. Also, the initial purchase price is high. If you, however, are disciplined in buying in bulk the ingredients needed to make multigrain bread and will plan ahead and make it every time you need a loaf, then you should buy a bread machine. If you can't do these things, and can take advantage of a sale such as the one I see often, the bread machine will be an unnecessary expense.

But often we just want the scrumptious taste of warm, freshly baked bread. If you can afford the expense of the machine for this purpose alone, then go for it. I found a used bread machine at Goodwill for $8. It needed a new part that cost me $15. All together, it was worth the purchase.

If you decide to buy one, make sure you have the feature that allows the bread to be air cooled after baking. Without this feature, your bread will become soggy unless removed from the oven within a few minutes after baking.

COFFEE

Coffee has become a trend for some and a necessity for others. I enjoy the brown liquid and was a deep connoisseur for a long time. I went so far as to have the beans imported from Hawaii because I felt these were the best-tasting beans in the world. I think I have tried them all.

Some readers will be irritated that I have even dedicated this much space and energy to coffee. But I do so because it is such a trend in the cities. Coffee shops are fun places to gather with friends, and many folks, like me, love that Java bean. And much of the time their coffee does taste better than home-brewed. But I hope to offer some suggestions to make your coffee taste as good as theirs and to save you many dollars in the process.

To cut down on the cost of drinking coffee, I have tried these ideas—some of which may appeal to you, others may not:

- If you think coffee tastes better at one of those trendy places, you're probably right. Your coffeemaker at home does not get the water as hot as their commercial machines do. The extra heat gives the coffee more flavor. If you desire to get that cup of coffee as close to theirs as possible, try boiling water in a kettle and manually pouring the water over the grounds.

- To get the most flavor from your beans, don't grind them until you are ready to brew. Even though coffee stays fresh for two to three weeks in the refrigerator, freeze the rest of the beans for optimum flavor. And remember that the finer the grind of coffee, the stronger the brew.

- If you brew coffee every day, some people recommend reusing coffee grounds once by putting the used ones in the fridge, then adding an equal amount of fresh grounds before brewing. This reduces the coffee expense but won't improve the flavor.

- Buy the expensive coffee filters and use them twice. Since they are made better, they can handle the wear. Better yet, buy the reusable type. They are made from either nylon or gold. They last for years and years (probably your lifetime), and will prove to be cheaper overall than paper filters. I bought a nylon one and have had it for thirteen years. It is dishwasher safe and can be rinsed after each use. (The nylon does not affect the taste of the coffee.)

- Don't buy a cup of coffee (or ground coffee) at the gourmet coffee shops. It can cost twenty-five times more than making it at home! One lady called me and said she enjoyed her daily ritual of getting a café mocha and muffin at her gourmet coffee shop on the way to work. On the phone, we figured how much that was costing her—a whopping $100 per month. At home she could do it for $5 per month. When she wondered about the time she was "saving," we figured she could make it herself in less time than it took to stop at the shop.

As much as I like the trendy atmosphere of these coffee places, I prefer to save money and time by making a premium cup myself. I love the taste of freshly brewed coffee, so I have learned to make a cup as strong as the shops do, and to make it at the time I want to drink it. If coffee sits on a warming plate for fifteen minutes, it has already become bitter. Reheated coffee just doesn't taste that good to me, so I make it only when I want to drink it. Freeze leftover coffee in ice cube trays and use in iced coffee drinks.

𝒟ECORATING

Decorating your home can be limited when you live on a tight budget. Several books have been dedicated to this fine art, showing us that a lack of money does not mean our homes have to look tacky. Check your local library for these. Here are some ideas I have learned to spruce things up:

Curtains

Buy a good heavy curtain from a thrift store, regardless of the print. Then find a bed sheet in a pattern you like. (Shop sales, thrift stores, or bedding outlets, and buy several.) The curtains I bought were a perfect fit for a full-sized sheet. Some may be the same size as two full-sized sheets sewn together. Wash the curtains in cold water and fluff-dry or line-dry for minimum shrinkage. Take out any bunching or pleating but leave the hems on the edges intact. The curtain should resemble a large rectangle. Sew the sheet around the edges of the curtain to cover the curtain. (A sheet alone would be too sheer.) Reapply any pleats and hang. Hem bottom of curtains after hanging. My six living room curtains cost a total of $55.

Valances

Using a 2 × 4 piece of wood, cut it to the width of your window. Sew fabric of your choice into a tube (twice the length of the board) and ease it onto the board. Fix it to the top of the window trim or nail to the wall above the window.

Furniture

Aside from bargain-hunting at garage sales and watching advertisements, furniture can be an expensive addition to the household. One family I know builds their own furniture. They find furniture manufacturers or staircase makers and take the scraps of wood left from their projects. Usually the wood is given free of charge as long as they pick it up. My friend's latest project is an armoire entertainment center. It is made of solid oak scraps. The total cost was less than $20 for hinges and supplies.

If you need to purchase furniture, don't be afraid to negotiate the price. Do some research on prices at other stores and show competitive ads to the salesperson. Make sure items are exactly the same. Tell the salesperson what you can afford and be sincere. This tactic got us many upgrades on a sofa sleeper. With each delay in the arrival of our order, we asked for another upgrade to compensate for our inconvenience. We got a superior mattress, fabric protection, and free delivery.

Sofa Recovering

If you have a fine sofa, but the covering has had it from all those little feet and spilled bottles, here is a creative idea. Find some fabric you like. For this you can again use a sheet, or buy a heavier fabric at an upholstery fabric outlet store. They have the ends of fabric rolls used by furniture stores. Or visit *www.fabric.com* to purchase fabric at very low prices. Remove the old fabric in sections with a razor edge and use these pieces as the pattern (add two inches to each side for tucking and mistakes). Attach the new fabric to the existing seams with a staple gun. Our love seat cost me $60 to redo myself. I was quoted $500 to have it done by someone else.

PERSONAL CARE

Hair Cuts, Shampoo

Most of us have to have our hair cut. How can we save here? Many people go to the thrifty cutting places like Supercuts, Great

Clips, or Cost Cutters. Others have discovered the beauty colleges near them. They charge very little and you are helping out a student.

Another idea is to find someone in your circle of friends and neighbors who does a fair job of cutting hair. If they are uncomfortable charging you for it, since they are probably unlicensed, try trading services. Exchange some haircuts for a sewing project or another task you do well.

This savings can really add up. If a family of four gets a haircut on the average of every six weeks, they are spending the following each year:

Trendy Salon	$35/cut	$1,260/yr.
Discount store	$9/cut	$324/yr.
Beauty college	$5/cut	$180/yr.
Trading services		$0/yr.
Do-it-yourself		$0/yr.
Let it grow		$0/yr.

We saved $60 per month by doing haircuts ourselves. The do-it-yourself option is easier than you think. Books can show you how to cut hair. There are even lessons available on videotape at the library. Practice on your kids first. Their hair grows fast and is usually messy from playing anyway.

To clean hair, ask yourself if you really need those expensive shampoos. Probably not. You can buy shampoo for under a dollar. This happens more often than you think—just watch the ads. For deep conditioning, I warm a little olive oil and leave it on my hair, then shampoo.

Cosmetics

Cosmetics are expensive, causing many frugally minded women to skip them altogether. There are, however, some ways to purchase good cosmetics at a discount, making them affordable for many. The first thing to explore is the generic or store-brand version of famous cosmetics. Some come in a close second to the original. To help you decide which brands are best for you (without having to buy several to try), read the book *Don't Go to the Cosmetics Counter Without Me*, by Paula Begoun. The author reviews the quality of most drugstore cosmetics.

If store brands are not for you, the best way to purchase name-brand cosmetics at a discount is through catalogs. Most of the large cosmetic manufacturers sell the remainder of a certain lot or color to surplus houses. These surplus products are sold for up to 90 percent off retail. Below are a few companies that offer free catalogs.

> Luzier Cosmetics
> 7910 Troost Ave.
> Kansas City, MO 64131-1920
> (800) 821-1920
>   Offers cosmetics
>
> Beauty Boutique
> P.O. Box 94519
> Cleveland, OH 44101-4503
> (440) 826-3008
>   Offers products from various name-brand cosmetic manu-
> facturers
>
> Essential Products Company, Inc.
> 90 Water Street
> New York, NY 10005
> (212) 344-4288
>   Offers copies of name-brand perfumes
>
> Classique Perfumes
> 139-01 Archer Avenue
> Jamaica, NY 11435
> (718) 657-8200
>   Offers copies of name-brand perfumes

You can also shop on the Internet for brand-name cosmetics at discount prices. One site that offers discounts is *www.cosmeticmall.com.*

$\mathcal{V}$ACATIONS

Plan ahead for your trip and save for it. If you can only save $500, don't take a $900 vacation. Stay within the range of what you can afford. Save what you didn't spend on groceries; send in for rebates; do some baby-sitting or other odd jobs. It doesn't matter how small the money is. Stash it away in a savings account. I have banked as little as $2, but I am faithful about saving whatever I can. One year at the end of nine months I had put away $700.

To keep the cost down for a vacation, don't pay for it with credit cards. Unless you can pay off the entire balance when the bill arrives, the finance charges could add hundreds of dollars to the cost of your trip.

Eating in restaurants is a drain on vacation cash. I try to eat in the motel room as often as possible and save the cash for fun outings. I get a room with a small refrigerator and keep food in it. We have cereal in the morning, sandwiches at lunch, and a frozen meal for dinner (if there is a microwave in the room). Since I can't cook a meal from scratch, a frozen dinner is the next best bargain. A frozen dinner costs three times less than eating out. Also many hotels offer a free continental breakfast and/or a family happy hour with hors d'oeuvres. This provision can often be a meal in itself.

What you pay for a room can vary greatly, so you must search out the best deals. Many hotels offer special rates on surplus rooms. (Not all rooms are booked at all times, and these are the discounted rooms.) But you have to ask if they have this type of discount. If you book a few months in advance, you're more likely to receive these discounts. If you are a member of a travel club such as AAA, you can also get a substantial discount. Again, you have to ask if they offer this discount. These two discounts saved us $150 on our last trip. And don't forget to use any entertainment book discounts that apply. The last time I traveled, I found that with our entertainment book's discount I could get a room at the Wyndham (four star) for the price of a Friendship Inn (three star).

There are other discounts available on travel arrangements. Our local warehouse club offers 5 percent cash back on any airline or Amtrak ticket purchase done through them. This means you can find the best bargain and then get another 5 percent off. Several grocery stores also offer discounts on airline tickets with a certain amount of grocery receipt totals. This can be profitable for you only if you were already going to spend that amount at that store.

Don't turn your nose up at top airlines just because you need to save money. I learned about a special that one of the most expensive airlines was offering just by calling to see what their prices were. It turned out their special fare was less than any of the best deals on any other airline. These deals aren't advertised; you have to ask. And don't overlook the use of the Internet. It provides much information on competitive rates. Web sites such as *Priceline.com, Excite.com,* and *Travelocity.com* offer searches for competitive airlines and hotel and car rental rates.

When making an airline reservation, pay for your ticket as soon as possible. The prices can (and do) go up. But don't be in such a hurry to get the ticket that you make a mistake in the travel plans. Any changes will incur a penalty charge. Ask if any discounts apply, such as staying over a Saturday night or flying midweek.

The use of credit cards is best when purchasing travel arrangements (airline, train, or package deals). Many credit card companies offer insurance for yourself, your luggage, and even canceled trips. Check with your card carrier. But make sure you can pay the balance off when you return.

If you are going to be gone a long time, you will need to park your car somewhere (unless you can get someone to drop you off and pick you up). Here are your options:

- Have a shuttle pick you up—$12 per person each way (this might be more expensive in your area).
- Park in the airport's long-term parking—about $8 per day.
- Before traveling, stay overnight in a motel nearby—free parking (they usually offer low rates and free shuttle to and from the airport).

Car rental rates vary widely. There are always deals to be found. Full price should not be in your contract. Get what you need (size, air-conditioning, etc.) and then review your options. Certain days of the week are cheaper. Returning at certain locations and on certain days can be cheaper. Filling up the tank as close to the return location as possible will be cheaper than paying the car rental agency to fill it up. And don't forget to check if you have a discount with an automobile club or entertainment book.

Rental car companies will offer you insurance when you rent a car. Your regular car insurance, however, may already cover you, making additional insurance a waste of money. Before you rent, check the coverage your own insurance company offers on rental cars. Make sure they cover injury as well as theft and collision. Some rental companies combine theft with collision. If you decline, theft of the car could be your responsibility.

This section covers some basic travel tips. For a more thorough discussion of how to save on vacations, please read the chapter dedicated to traveling in my book *Frugal Families—Making the Most of Your Hard-Earned Money*.

TOOLS AND APPLIANCES

Many Americans have gadgets for this function and that. And many of these items are only used two or three times a year. Try going in with a neighbor or relative on a tool or piece of equipment that will be seldom used. Or better yet, borrow or rent it from a hardware store if you can. This applies to items like canning equipment, spray painters, fruit pickers, or special ladders.

If you think you will use a tool more than two or three times a year, start shopping at garage sales. I got a great belt sander for $20.

When those large appliances break down, such as a washer or dryer, look at buying a refurbished one instead of repairing yours. Many refurbished appliances cost no more than $99. That's close to the cost of the labor alone in a repair job. Most local newspapers list companies that buy and sell used appliances.

If an appliance is truly ready for the dump, don't pay someone else to take it away. Call one of the refurbishing companies to see if they will take it at no charge. They will use it for the parts they pull from it.

PAINTS, VARNISH, CEMENT

By looking around (not in dumpsters or garbage piles), I have been able to obtain paint, cement stones for my garden, and drywall for our house project free of charge. Much of what we throw out is not garbage but surplus. Usually it's something we don't want to store.

As my mom used to say, "You won't know until you ask." Well, she was right. Whenever I see construction taking place near my home, I wait until they are done. Then I ask what they will do with the leftover wood, cement, or paint. If it is a small job, the workers are usually glad to give it to you. Otherwise they would have to go to the dump and pay to dispose of it.

There was some repair being done to the sidewalk in front of our home. Watching it proved to be educational and fun for the kids. When they were done, they were going to throw out the excess cement. We brought pans and buckets and asked them to pour it into them. We made handprints in the cement, stuck shells to it, and wrote on the surfaces. We have some unique garden stones that cost us nothing. I have seen stepping stone kits in catalogs for $26 that would produce nothing more than what we accomplished with the free cement.

One person recommended stopping by the local recycling center to pick up free half-used cans of varnish, paint, or paint remover. I personally am not comfortable with this plan. We don't know how old the containers are or if chemicals have been mixed together.

*L*EGAL ADVICE

Sometimes we have legal questions about something we are doing, but we don't want to pay the fee for the help. I'm not talking about when you are in an accident or being sued. I'm talking about that free-lance job you may want to look into, but you don't know what to charge or if you need a contract. Or that magazine article you want to sell, but you can't understand the contract they sent you.

There are a few organizations that will help you for a small (or no) fee for thirty minutes of advice. One is called SCORE (Service Corps of Retired Executives), *www.score.org*, and is manned by small business veterans who are happy to answer your questions about what to charge on a free-lance job or how to start that small business in your garage. Another I found was Lawyers for the Arts. In California, they are called the California Lawyers for the Arts (*www.calawyersforthearts.org*). They offer thirty minutes of legal advice related to the arts (literary, performing, film) for a minimal fee. Most chambers of commerce can direct you to these services in your area.

CHECK CHARGES AND BANK FEES

Most of us write checks and have to pay for them. Theoretically we can write a check on toilet paper, but each banking corporation has the right to refuse processing this form of "promissory note." Banks offer to sell you checks, but at a premium. We can go directly to the check manufacturers and save about half of what a bank would charge. The best deals come from Current (800) 426-0822, *www.currentchecks.com*, and Checks in the Mail (800) 733-4443, *www.citm.com*. The first set of 200 checks is usually $4.95, and future orders are $6.95 (these are for plain checks). I have used Current for many years and know I have saved enough for a weekend vacation just by using this one source.

For most of us bank fees are a necessary evil. Lately the banks want to charge for everything and then some. I am charged if I go inside the bank to a teller window instead of using the ATM. Other banks charge for using the ATM as well. There are some ways to lower the bank fees. Ask your bank what discounts it offers. Our bank offers a $1 discount per month for each of these: payroll direct deposit, ATM use only, and canceled checks on file at the bank. I also can get the entire monthly fee waived if I keep a minimum amount in the account all month. Sometimes a savings account may be more cost effective if you don't use checks often and can conduct business with cash from the savings account. Credit unions are sometimes cheaper, if you can join one.

LONG-DISTANCE PHONE CARRIERS

There are so many long-distance carriers that it can be confusing to choose. Many of us don't switch because we don't understand who offers a better deal. The best deal will differ from home to home. A leading carrier that many friends claimed was the cheapest was not the cheapest for my family. Our calling habits, times, and locations were different from many homes. To do an accurate comparison, write down your calling habits. Are most calls to one area? Do you call at certain times of the day or week? With these needs in mind, call around and get quotes. Don't forget to factor in any monthly fees they charge. We found that paying a flat fee per minute with no monthly fees was cheaper at the end of the month for us. Below are some of the carriers that I reviewed. There are many more small carriers available than I have listed. We have found that the last one on the list (C-Com) is the cheapest. Check it out for yourself!

AT&T . . . . (800) 222-0300
MCI . . . . (800) 444-3333
Lifeline-Amerivision . . . . (800) 800-7550
    (offers 10% of your total bill to charity of your choice)
Excel . . . . (800) 875-9235
C-Com . . . . (303) 938-1417

To help you wade through carrier rates, a group called TRAC has compiled a listing of long-distance rates. For a copy, send five dollars with a SASE to Box 27279, Washington, D.C. 20005 (*www.trac.org*).

Another way to save on long distance is to use the Internet. There are a few Web sites that allow you to make calls for free! Calls are made over the Internet via their Web site. All that is required from you is a microphone, or preferably a headset with an earpiece and microphone. The person on the other end uses her phone. You dial your call on the site and talk through them. There may be some lag time between when you talk and when the other party hears you, but for the most part it works well. Some sites charge a small fee for international calls. A few well-known sites that offer this free service are *www.net2phone.com*, *www.dialpad.com*, and *www.freewebcall.com*. For a review of these and other sites like them, please visit *www.1st-free-long-distance.com*.

Seasonal Savings

Almost everything we need for our homes goes on sale at some time during the year. On the next two pages is a chart of when things typically go on sale. Your area may vary as to what is on sale at what time of year, but there should be some similarity. Modify the chart for yourself as you see variations.

JANUARY–FEBRUARY

(white sale, Presidents' Day sale)

- *Clothes:* men's shirts
- *Linens:* towels, linens, sheets
- *Appliances:* stock clearance, clothes dryers, used cars, water heaters
- *Household:* weatherizing treatments, art supplies, bicycles, books, curtains
- *Furniture*
- *Gifts:* Christmas wrap and ornaments, toys, etc.
- *Groceries:* meats (turkey, ham), baking items

MARCH

(end of winter sale, pre-spring sale)

- *Clothes:* coats, clothes for all, shoes
- *Appliances:* TVs, housewares, washing machines
- *Household:* ski equipment
- *Groceries:* artichokes

APRIL–MAY

(after-Easter sale, pre-summer sale, Mother's Day sale, Memorial Day sale)

- *Clothes:* dresses, suits, coats, summer clothes
- *Linens:* towels
- *Appliances:* TVs, tires
- *Household:* outdoor furniture, paint, tools, garden supplies, camping and boating equipment
- *Gifts:* gift items
- *Groceries:* artichokes, dairy products, ham, eggs, chicken

JUNE–JULY

(Father's Day sale, end-of-school sale, after-July 4 sale)

- *Clothes:* summer clothes, shoes
- *Appliances:* air conditioners
- *Household:* school supplies, outdoor furniture, building materials
- *Furniture:* most furniture
- *Gifts:* gift items
- *Groceries:* dairy products, fresh fish, barbecue foods

AUGUST–SEPTEMBER

(end-of-summer sale, pre-fall sale, Labor Day sale)

- *Clothes:* summer clothes, fall clothes, school clothes, swimwear
- *Household:* school supplies, garden supplies and tools, outdoor furniture, rugs and carpets, car batteries and mufflers, bicycles
- *Groceries:* fresh fish, lamb, canned goods

OCTOBER

- *Household:* summer sports equipment, cars from dealerships (buy close to the last day of the month for the best deal)

NOVEMBER

- *Clothes:* men's shirts
- *Appliances:* water heaters
- *Household:* home improvement supplies, homes are cheaper
- *Groceries:* spices (stock up!)

DECEMBER

Not a good time to buy anything until December 26.

RESOURCES

The Best Bargain Family Vacations in the U.S.A., Laura Sutherland (St. Martin's Griffin, 1997).

Decorating on a Shoestring: You Can Create a Beautiful Home, Gwen Ellis and Jo Ann Janssen (Broadman & Holman Publishers, 1999).

Don't Go to the Cosmetics Counter Without Me, Paula Begoun (Beginning Press, 2000).

Free Vacations and Bargain Adventures in the U.S.A., Evelyn Kaye (Blue Penguin Publications, 1995).

To Make Your Car Last a Lifetime, Bob Fendell (Holt, Rinehart, and Winston, 1981).

U.S.A. 2000: The Budget Travel Guide, Caroline Ball and Barbara Rogers (Globe Pequot Press, 1999).

CHAPTER TWENTY-SEVEN

Medical Expenses

$ $ $

*M*edicine has become a big business, and we need to start learning how to play the game. It used to be that if you were sick you saw a doctor. Now it's imperative to know who you see, what services are provided, and at what rate. Let's learn a few tricks to help reduce the expenses of illness. Please remember that the advice I share is lay advice and should never be substituted for any professional health care advice.

*M*EDICAL INSURANCE

Many people make a superficial decision when choosing an insurance carrier. Some choose one type of plan simply because they prefer the ease of a co-payment rather than submitting an insurance bill for a refund. Our decision for our care should go beyond convenience. We should look at the type of care we'll receive as well as the annual costs between carriers.

The first thing to remember is that you need insurance. Many families I know don't have it because they are mostly healthy or they can't afford it. One accident or illness could wipe them out or have them at other people's doors asking for financial help. Another reason to carry it is that you will always be treated better if you have insurance. Many doctors and hospitals won't provide care or will provide it with less quality and attention than for insured patients.

When I shop for insurance, the first thing I consider is the type of care I want. Is it important to me to have a doctor I know and that I can see each time I need to? Will I get the best testing done for a problem I encounter? Can I go where I think I need to? The answers to these will direct you to the type of carrier you should choose. An HMO (Health Maintenance Organization) will provide you with "managed" care. This means that the doctors (and not you) decide when you need further tests, and they decide who does them. Some HMOs are more controlling than others, not allowing you to see the doctor of your choice. Some allow you to select the doctor of your choice, but then require that you stay within his/her clinic for all other medical needs. The thing to remember about this type of insurance carrier is that the more control they have over your care, the lower your medical premium will be. This is because they decide what care you get, and they save money if they provide less care.

We have switched insurance providers a few times over the years. We usually did this for cost reduction: switching insurance companies, but keeping our doctor, to reduce our premiums and overall out-of-pocket expenditures. Once we switched to a more expensive carrier. Even though our monthly premiums went up by $165, the overall out-of-pocket expenditures at year-end were less.

We made this change when we discovered that my husband had cancer. We had caught it at an early stage and had the freedom to wait six months to begin treatment. We decided to use that time to get him as healthy as possible with diet and exercise. We also used that time to wait for the next insurance open enrollment period through his employer. That allowed us to switch to an indemnity insurance carrier—one that allows you to see any doctor you want while you pay an annual deductible, plus 30 percent of the bill. We wanted the freedom to go anywhere we wished. There was a fairly new treatment for his type of cancer that the local doctors didn't know how to perform. The option that was available locally was invasive and carried more severe side effects. The option we wanted to pursue was available out of state. If we had not waited to change carriers, we would have been limited to our town's HMO plan and their treatment options. Sometimes paying a higher monthly premium pays in the long run.

After you decide which type of insurance is right for you and your family, you should then start doing some comparative shopping. The most accessible and the cheapest place to buy insurance is through your employer or your spouse's employer.

If you have no employer policy available, look at any professional groups that you belong to: your college's alumni association, your automobile insurance carrier, or any school you may be attending. Buying a policy as an individual will cost you 15 to 40 percent more than with a group. There are also companies such as Blue Cross Blue Shield that sell directly to individuals. There are groups of people who form their own insurance group by pooling their money. The families accepted must all adhere to certain lifestyles and health requirements (such as no smoking, drinking, drugs) to participate.

When you purchase medical insurance, estimate what your medical needs will be during the next year. List what you needed last year. Then consider things such as the types of hospital services you may need, surgeries, prescriptions, ambulance, well-baby care, maternity, physical therapy, out-of-town coverage, chronic illness coverage, and any annual cap on what you will spend. Then factor in the potential carrier's portion. By doing this sort of evaluation, we saved $300 per year.

Once you have selected a carrier, find out about their policy on visits to urgent care facilities and emergency rooms. One type of service might be covered at a very different rate than the other. Also some carriers restrict the coverage of certain types of visits to urgent care facilities and emergency rooms and might even refuse to pay.

A few more things to remember when choosing insurance:

- Don't always assume that cheaper is better. Check out the reputation of the carrier. Make sure the company you pick has a high rating. See how Best Insurance Reports rates them or research ratings on the Internet.
- Don't under-insure yourself or your family. Make sure you will be covered for major things.
- Pay as high a deductible as you can. You want to only pay for coverage of losses that you can't afford. The higher the deductible, the lower the payments.

*H*OSPITALS

Most people assume that a doctor or hospital bill is a fixed fee. In many cases it is, but not always. Many doctors are very understanding and will accept whatever the insurance company will cover combined with whatever you are able to pay. Many large bills can be negotiated, especially if the hospital is in a lower-income area. These hospitals have many customers who simply can't pay for their visits, so the hospital has to write off the cost. If a customer can pay, but needs to make small payments, they usually cooperate in order to get the money eventually.

My husband had to spend three days in intensive care at a hospital in a lower-income part of a city. When all of the various bills arrived (there were twelve in all), we could only afford to pay each at $10 per month. All of them (except the hospital) were willing to accept these terms, and none ever charged interest.

On a separate trip to a hospital a few years later, we landed in a wealthier part of town. This four-hour hospital stay cost more than our three-day visit to intensive care at the other hospital. This hospital did not want to accept payments. Instead, they offered us a 20 percent discount if we paid by the end of that month. That added up to a large savings and was worth doing what we had to in order to pay it.

Don't be afraid to contest the amount that the insurance company decides to cover. There are people with tender hearts working at these companies. I have had medications and procedures covered that normally would not be because I wrote a sincere and explanatory letter regarding the situation. Send supporting documents, such as a doctor's letter, if you can.

*D*OCTOR BILLS

When you finally use your insurance, find ways to reduce the expense of the bill. Use the carrier's preferred doctors and save 40 percent. Ask the carrier how else you can reduce your part of the bill. Some doctors will write off your portion of the bill if you show financial need.

Use the phone as often as possible instead of making an appointment. Many doctors will advise you and even prescribe something over the phone. You can save $50 by letting your fingers do the walking.

Check out what your local county board of health has to offer. Many offer immunizations for children for free or for a minimal fee of $5. A visit to the doctor for the same service runs $75 or more.

$\mathcal{M}$EDICATIONS

When buying prescription or over-the-counter drugs, go for the generic version as often as possible. This can save you 30 to 80 percent compared to the cost of its name-brand equivalent. And even generic or store-brand versions of the same drug can vary greatly in price. One store's own brand of aspirin may be much cheaper than another store's. Comparing prices is essential. And don't fear the quality. There are strict controls on the production of medications, so one brand has to be made exactly like another in order to be called by the same chemical name (e.g., ibuprofen).

Don't overlook mail-order pharmacies, such as AbeeWell Virtual Pharmacy, (888) 2-BEEWELL; Action Mail Order, (800) 452-1976; and America's Pharmacy, (800) 247-1003. These are great for medications you use regularly. They can give a good discount: up to 60 percent off name-brand prescriptions. If you have access to AARP (American Association of Retired Persons), they have arranged good pricing as well. Contact their pharmacy for details at (800) 456-2277.

For those who have no prescription insurance plan, there is a program that might help. Most major drug manufacturers offer drugs for little or no fee to those who cannot afford to purchase them. Each company has different requirements for receiving free prescription drugs, but all require a doctor's application on your behalf. If your doctor is unfamiliar with the program, have him/her contact the Pharmaceutical Manufacturers Association at (202) 835-3400.

When one of us has a cold, I avoid the combination remedies. There is usually some drug in there we don't need, and they tend to be more expensive than the individual ingredients combined—as much as 20 to 30 percent more. Any time you buy medicine, compare the unit price (the cost per milliliter or milligram). Sometimes it's cheaper to take two capsules of a lesser dose than to take one of a larger dose. This is particularly true of aspirin and other pain-killers.

We keep several separate drugs in the cabinet—one for each type of symptom. When I have a particular symptom, I take only the drug appropriate for that symptom. Some people like the hot flu medication drink that is packaged for your convenience. Instead, take what you need (fever reducer, decongestant, antihistamine) and have a hot cup of herb tea or hot water with lemon juice and honey. The same effect will be achieved and it will cost you much less. Following is a list of drugs and their indicated purpose. This should make shopping for the right remedy a bit easier and help you avoid taking drugs you don't need.

Generic Names and Purposes for Cold Medications

Name	Purpose
dextromethorphan	for dry cough/cough suppressant
guaifenesin	for productive or "gooey" cough/ expectorant
pseudoephedrine	decongestant
ephedrine	decongestant
chlorpheniramine	antihistamine
diphenhydramine	antihistamine

It's important to know what you need. You can complicate your problems by using the wrong drug. For example, if you have a productive cough, using a cough suppressant isn't a good idea. Ask your doctor or pharmacist before you self-medicate to be sure you're choosing the right medicine.

When shopping for vitamins, the same guidelines apply. Know what elements you need and shop around for the best generic price. Don't forget to check the expiration dates as well. To know if you are getting a good manufacturer of the tablet, try this quick test. Drop a tablet in a few teaspoons of any kind of vinegar (to simulate stomach acid) and leave it for forty-five minutes (you can stir it once in a while to simulate stomach churning). It should break apart or dissolve by the end of the experiment. If it doesn't, then the manufacturer packs it too tightly or adds too many fillers, and it passes through you unabsorbed. I tested all of my vitamins and found one of mine that didn't dissolve. All the time that I took them, I wasn't getting any benefit from them. I wrote to the manufacturer and received a full refund. If you would like to know which brands of multivitamins are more complete, check the library for recent articles that review the most popular brand of vitamins. One newsletter with a good vitamin review is the *Nutrition Action Health Letter* written by the Center for Science in the Public Interest, 1875 Connecticut Ave, NW, Suite 300, Washington, D.C. 20009-5728, (202) 332-9110, *www.cspinet.org*.

DENTAL EXPENSES

The best way to avoid dental work is to take care of your teeth: brush, floss, avoid sweets, and have regular cleanings and exams. Thirty-five percent of all gum disease and tooth loss is caused by plaque. A root canal can cost hundreds of dollars per tooth. You can buy a lot of dental floss, toothpaste, and toothbrushes for that kind of money.

Dental schools offer low-cost cleanings, exams, and dental work. They charge 50-75 percent less than a private dentist. Certified dentists always supervise the students. If you cannot afford any amount, or there is no dental school near you, check with your local county health department. Many offer low-cost dental services.

RESOURCES

How to Cut Your Medical Bills, Art Ulene (Ulysses Press, 1994), out of print; check library for copy.

The Savvy Medical Consumer, Charles B. Inlander (Peoples' Medical Society, 1997).

Stay Well Without Going Broke: Winning the War Over Medical Bills, Pattie Vargas (Unknown, 1994).

Winning the Insurance Game, Ralph Nader (Doubleday, 1993).

CHAPTER TWENTY-EIGHT

Utilities

$ $ $

$\mathcal{O}$ur utility bill was another item in our budget, like groceries, that fluctuated. That meant we could make some changes and perhaps save money. With some research and a few simple changes, we were able to reduce our overall utility bill by 25 percent.

First, we had a free energy audit on our home by our local utility company. Some areas charge a fee for this service. They reviewed our usage patterns over the past year and made recommendations for energy savings.

The most enlightening information was how much energy each appliance was costing. This determined the order that I was going to work on our energy expenses. Following is a chart that shows the energy use of most common household appliances. I based the cost on the kilowatt per hour that each uses and the energy rate for our area. It is meant as a general guideline for your expenses.

For a more accurate determination of the costs you are incurring, have your local utility company explain your rates or perform an energy audit.

Energy Use Chart

Appliance	Estimated Energy Cost*
Water Heater	
Electric	$50–$65 per month
Gas	$13–$20 per month
Refrigerator	
Frost-free—6 cubic feet	$19.50 per month
Frost-free—20 cubic feet	$23.40 per month
Manual defrost—10 cubic feet	$8 per month
Frost-free—side-by-side	$26–$39 per month
Freezer	
Frost-free—15 cubic feet	$20 per month
Manual defrost—15 cubic feet	$12 per month
Washing Machine (full load)	
Cold water only	$.16 per load
Warm wash, cold rinse	$.23 per load
Hot wash, warm rinse	$.36 per load
Clothes Dryer	
Electric	$.70 per load
Gas	$.16 per load
Central Heating	
Furnace—small home	$16–$40 per month ($.40 per hour)
Furnace—large home	$40–$200 per month
Electric—small home	$55–$110 per month
Electric—large home	$110–$400 per month
Central Cooling	
Window air-conditioner	$25–$75 per month
Central air-conditioner	$74–$220 per month
Electric blanket	$2.10–$4 per month
Dishwasher	
Gas water heater	$.23 per load

*Based on a cost of 13¢ per kwh. Your rates may vary. Most of this information came from my local utility company.

Electric water heater	$.49 per load
Oven	
Gas	$.06 per hour
Electric	$.16 per hour
Range-top burner	
Gas	$.04 per hour
Electric	$.15 per hour
Toaster oven	$.06 per hour
Microwave oven	$.15 per hour
Electric frying pan	$.13 per hour
Lighting	
Incandescent bulb, 100 watts	$.01 per hour
Fluorescent bulb, 27 watts	$.0025 per hour
Computer	$.01–$.02 per hour
Television, color	$.02–$.06 per hour
Television, black and white	$.01 per hour
VCR	$.01 per hour
Radio	$.008 per hour
Stereo	$.02 per hour
Toaster	$.01 per use
Vacuum cleaner	$.10 per hour
Iron	$.13 per hour

COST-SAVING MEASURES

Here are some changes that can be easily implemented in most homes.

Water Heater

Turning down the temperature of your water heater saves more than you think. For every ten degrees that you turn the heater down, you can save 6 to 10 percent of its energy costs. Most energy advisors recommend that you not turn the temperature below 120°. Many automatic dishwashers require a minimum temperature of 120° in order to function properly. Check your dishwashing manual for specific requirements.

Many people wash their dishes by hand in order to save hot water. Depending on how you hand wash your dishes, it may cost you more to wash by hand. If you run the water for each dish to be rinsed, you may be using more hot water than an automatic dishwasher. For maximum savings, fill one basin for washing and one basin for rinsing and turn the water off.

The water heater's location is key to its best performance. If it is far from the appliances that use it most (like in a garage), much of the energy is wasted as the water travels through the pipes. You can waste 10 to 15 percent of the energy used to heat the water by having it travel. If moving the water heater is too costly, insulate the pipes that carry the water to the appliances.

For other ways to reduce the costs of your water heater, try these:

- Wrap the heater in a special insulating blanket.
- Install an appliance timer that turns the water heater off during nonuse hours (like sleeping hours and vacations).
- Reduce the use of hot water where you can—showering accounts for 30 percent of hot water use in most homes; laundry accounts for 14 percent.
- Don't use the rinse/hold function on your dishwasher. Rinse them yourself, in cold water.
- If you need to replace the water heater, make sure the new one has a high energy efficiency rating. Even if other water heaters are cheaper, the higher energy efficiency rating will pay off.

Water

Since fresh water is only a small percentage of the water available on this planet, we need to use it wisely. Saving money is another good motivator. I have lived through two drought periods and can never go back to wasting water the way I used to. Many of us don't realize how much we are using.

Outdoors, much of our water is lost to evaporation. We put mulch around the plants and trees to trap the moisture in the ground. We timed sprinklers to go on at night so that little was lost to heat. We replaced our kids' sprinkler games with squirt-gun games. We wash the car with a nozzle that shuts off between uses. We don't wash the patio if we can sweep it instead.

Indoors, we try to double on baths for the littlest kids. They don't get too dirty and can either share a bath or use the tub one after the other. We wash clothes only when they need it. Some folks find it easier to throw clothes in the hamper than to hang them up at the end of the day.

If you don't have a low-flow toilet, you can create one. Fill a two-liter plastic jug (soda bottle) with water and sink it in the toilet tank. This will reduce the amount of water used with each flush.

We like baths but know that showers save on water usage. A shower uses four times less water than a bath. And a low-flow showerhead can save you another 40 percent on water usage. A tub with less water will be as thrifty as a shower. A long shower probably costs as much as a full tub.

The dishwasher uses 10 to 15 gallons of water per washing, so only run it when needed and when full. Don't use the rinse/hold function when you can rinse them yourself before loading.

Here are some more ideas for water savings:

- When taking a shower, wet yourself, turn the water off, wash, then turn the water on to rinse.
- Don't let the water run while brushing teeth or shaving.
- Fix any leaking faucets and running toilets. These can lead up to dozens of gallons wasted per day.
- Install aerators on all faucets.
- Don't use running water to thaw frozen meat. Let meat sit in cold water instead.
- Run the washing machine with full loads only.

Laundry

Most of the expenses of doing laundry come from creating heat—the heat of the water and the heat of the dryer. You can reduce the washing machine's energy usage by 90 percent by washing and rinsing in cold water only. The average cost of washing and drying a load of laundry is about $1 per load. That is based on a cold-water wash and an electric dryer.

To maximize the savings with your laundry, try these ideas:

- Always wash a full load. The cost of washing two medium loads does not equal one full load.
- Always dry a full load but don't overfill the dryer. Air needs to circulate between the clothes.
- Line dry whenever you can. Purchase a drying rack for indoor drying in the winter. Or stretch a couple of lines across the laundry room. To soften towels, run them in the dryer for a few minutes, then line dry.
- To cut down on ironing the more casual clothes, spray the clean and dry clothes with diluted fabric softener (¼ cup softener to 2 cups water), smooth with your hands, and hang on a hanger.
- Dry similar fabrics together so the dryer will quit sooner. One towel in a load of permanent-press clothes will keep the whole load running longer.
- Dry loads of clothes one after the other, capturing the heat already in the dryer.
- Make sure that the dryer vent is straight. A bent one will reduce airflow and dryer efficiency.
- Clean the lint trap after every load. Lint reduces airflow, and the dryer has to work harder to do the job.
- Check with your utility company for discounts on energy during off-peak hours. Only run the appliances during those hours to save even more.

Heating and Cooling

To efficiently heat a house, you must stop air from leaking in where it isn't welcome. Air leaks are one of the major wastes of energy. They usually cost you another 10 percent in energy costs. I found them around our doors and windows and in my fireplace damper. Anywhere two sections meet in a house (a wall and a window, a wall and a door, a vent and a ceiling) is a good place to check for an air leak. There are several easy ways to tell if there is a leak. The quickest way is to light a candle and slowly move it around the edges of the opening. If it flickers, there is an air leak. (Please be careful not to set the curtains on fire as you do this.) For a safer way, have someone blow air with a hair dryer around edges while you stand outside feeling for the air.

Once I found where my leaks were, I sealed them up with felt weather stripping found at most hardware stores. For some joints I used caulking. This is especially helpful outside for sealing around the joints between the walls and foundation, or the meeting of the brick and walls. For the fireplace, there are foam blocks you can buy to put in the damper door to seal any cracks. Check for fire hazards before using caulk or any permanent materials in the fireplace. The whole weatherizing treatment cost $15. My central heater used to go on four times per night, but now it only goes on one time per night, adding up to at least a 10 percent reduction in our energy bill.

Other ideas for reducing heating costs:

- Change or clean your heater's filter every month it is used. Dust gathers and makes the heater work harder to heat the rooms. This will save you 15 percent of your heating costs.
- Plant trees for sun and wind protection. Get a tree that sheds leaves (deciduous) in the winter so that it blocks sun on the house in the summer and lets the sun shine on the house in the winter. This could save you 10 to 30 percent in heating and cooling costs.
- Insulate your attic and walls to the highest R-value that your county building code recommends. This will reduce your heating costs by 20 to 30 percent.
- Close the damper on your fireplace after the ashes are cold. This could reduce your heating loss by 10 percent.
- Check if there is a draft or excessive heat (such as a fireplace) near the thermostat in the house. It may be kicking the heater/cooler on when the rest of the house is fine.
- Turn the thermostat down and wear more warm clothing. For every degree that you lower the thermostat, you save 3 percent on energy costs. (Use caution when turning down the heat if you are ill or elderly. It may not be medically advised, or in the case of the elderly, some can easily suffer hypothermia with minor temperature reduction.)
- Close off the vent and shut doors to rooms not being used.
- If you are moving to a new home, consider a bi-level house instead of a long ranch-style house. Heat escapes through the

roof, so the more roof surface you have, the more heat loss you will have.

- Consider an attic fan to suck the hot air out and circulate air in the house. These drop the temperature in a house by at least ten degrees with little energy usage. In the winter they can keep heating bills lower as well.
- Avoid using the fireplace for heating; 90 percent of the heat that a fire generates goes up the chimney. Fireplaces also tend to suck out the warm air inside the house. Install glass doors over the fireplace that will allow heat in but will not take heat out with the fire. Or invest in a stove insert that uses and distributes heat efficiently.
- If wood is plentiful and cheap in your area, and you have a fireplace stove, wood would be a cheaper source of heating than electricity or gas.

The Kitchen

The first thing I did to conserve energy in my kitchen was to get rid of the extra freezer I had. It wasn't actually in my kitchen (it was in the garage), but I considered it an extension of my kitchen, as it held all my extra food. When the energy audit revealed that it was responsible for 15 to 20 percent of my utility bill, I questioned its cost effectiveness. I figured it was costing $20 per month to run. I was buying in bulk and storing food in there, but the savings on bulk foods was being spent on the appliance to store them in. This seemed illogical. At that particular time we needed every dollar we could save, and $20 could help pay off another bill or pay for four or five meals.

I was determined to find a way to do without it. I made more frequent trips to the day-old bread store (or other outlets for special bulk purchases), instead of once a month. This way I didn't need to store as much food. I learned to freeze meals in plastic bags and lay them flat so the foods took up less room in the freezer. As I've said, I purchased a wire rack and created a shelf in the small freezer section of my refrigerator. This gave me more storage space. Once I was confident I could do without it, I sold the freezer.

When I cook, I can easily conserve energy with some minor

changes. When I bake, I try to bake several things at once so the oven is not heated for just one dish. For smaller dishes, the microwave or toaster oven is more energy efficient. I don't preheat the oven unless I am baking breads. I try not to peek at the foods while cooking, since I will lose as much as 20 percent of the heat trapped in there. If you have a self-cleaning oven, clean it right after you are finished baking. You are then using the heat already trapped in the oven. For maximum air circulation, make sure the racks in the oven are not covered with foil. Any blockage of the air movement means the oven will heat unevenly and give false temperature readings.

For range-top cooking, the pan should match the burner size. A small pan on a large burner will waste 40 percent of the heat generated. By using a lid on all pans, you can use three times less energy to cook a dish. Copper-bottomed pans heat up faster and require less energy to cook foods.

Other ideas for saving energy in the kitchen:

- If you have a choice between gas or electric ranges and ovens, the gas version will save you money. Do not consider remodeling for that reason, though, without having a professional compare the savings you will gain over the cost of the remodeling.
- A gas range/oven with an automatic ignition saves 40 to 50 percent more than a pilot light.
- Turn off the range or oven a few minutes before the food is done. Heat still remains on the burner or in the oven.
- Boil water on the range, not in the microwave oven. The microwave uses more energy to do the job, and they take about the same amount of time.
- Broiling is more energy efficient than baking.
- Check with your utility company for discounts on energy during off-peak hours. Only run the oven during those hours to save even more.
- In the summer, do your baking and dishwashing in the evening to avoid heating up the house. In the winter, do these activities in the morning (to help heat up the house).

Lighting

Most light bulbs are incandescent. These are inefficient makers of light. They use 10 percent of their energy for producing light, while 90 percent is wasted on the heat they produce. Fluorescent bulbs use 65 to 75 percent less energy to produce light, and they last ten times longer than incandescent bulbs. The Energy Use Chart earlier in this chapter can be deceptive when we talk about lighting costs. It says that we only spend one cent per hour on light bulbs that are turned on. We tend to forget how quickly this adds up. We usually have several bulbs on, and we tend to leave them on for several hours. This can add up to as much as 30 percent of your utility bill.

If converting your lighting fixtures to fluorescent isn't in your budget, try some of the fluorescent bulbs made to screw into lamp sockets. These can save wherever they fit. If you are stuck with incandescent bulb usage, try these ideas to reduce some of the costs:

- Clear light bulbs give off more light than frosted versions.
- Many bulbs can be replaced by lower wattage bulbs and still meet your lighting needs.
- When buying bulbs, don't go by the wattage. The lumens determine how much light is produced. Each bulb has a lumen number on it as well. For a brighter room, pick a higher number of lumens. For soft lighting, pick a lower lumen number.
- A light-colored lampshade will allow more light.
- Only light the area of a room where you are working or reading. The whole room doesn't need to be lit.
- Turn off lights when you leave a room.
- Avoid the long-life bulbs. They cost you more in the long run because they use more energy. Stick with less expensive lower-wattage bulbs.
- If you have fluorescent lights, don't turn them on and off frequently. That shortens the life of the bulb. Leave them on if you will return to the room soon.

RESOURCES

Consumer Guide to Home Energy Savings, Alex Wilson (American Council for an Energy-Efficient Economy, 2000).

Cut Your Electric Bills in Half, Ralph J. Herbert (Rodale Press, 1989), out of print; check library for copy.

547 Easy Ways to Save Energy in Your Home, Roger Albright (Garden
   Way Publishing, 1978), out of print; check library for copy.
Homemaker's Book of Energy Savers, Jean E. Laird (Macmillan, 1982),
   out of print; check library for copy.

CHAPTER TWENTY-NINE

Crafts for Kids

$ $ $

There are many days when my kids are asking for something
to do. I could buy a craft or some other toy, but I have found my
budget doesn't allow for those solutions. It's amazing what a little
imagination can do. When I lived in Nigeria and Pakistan, I saw
kids make toys out of things they found. They inspired me to be
less dependent on ready-made toys. I began researching ways to
make our crafts. My kids appreciate the time I have invested. The
cost is minimal, and we have fun together. Below are some ideas
we have enjoyed.

Kids' Aprons

I don't believe in buying a special apron for kids (unless it's
from a garage sale). Aprons are expensive and the kids outgrow
them quickly. Instead of a ready-made apron, we turn my husband's old long-sleeved shirts into paint and craft aprons. The
kids wear the shirts backward (so the buttons are in the back) with
the cuffs rolled up slightly. The shirts are long enough to cover
their clothes well.

Bubbles That Last

½ C. liquid Dawn or Joy
2 T. glycerin (at drugstores)
5 C. water

Pour water into container first. Add dish soap and glycerin and stir (try not to make it froth). Dip a bubble wand into the solution and blow!

Bubble wands: For homemade bubble wands, try bending wire into any shape (a coat hanger works). Provide adult supervision because of the sharp ends.

Bird Cookies

wooden tree ornaments or shapes (¼ inch thick)
peanut butter
birdseed
string

Punch a hole (using a nail and hammer) in the top of the shape and add a string loop. Slather wooden shapes with peanut butter. Roll in birdseed. Hang outside where you can watch the birds eat.

Bird Treats

½ C. peanut butter
½ C. flour
1½ C. birdseed

Mix well and shape into a ball. Press flat to ½ inch thick. Place on baking sheet. Gently poke a hole in the middle of the "cookie." Bake at 425° for 30 minutes. Cool completely. Hang with string outside.

How to Make Paper

This is not only a craft but also a lesson in recycling.

several pieces of paper (newspaper, binder paper, or even paper bags)
window screen on a wooden frame (screen can be bought at the hardware store, or art stores sell plain wooden frames to which you can staple screen)
bucket or other container to soak the paper
blender
magnifying glass
dry newspaper or felt

Tear the paper into small squares and soak in water several hours. Place ½ cup of paper in blender. Fill the blender with water from the bucket. Blend the paper for 30 seconds. Blending makes paper pulp. Put some pulp on your finger and look at it under the magnifying glass. There are tiny wood fibers.

Over a sink, spread the layer of pulp evenly onto the screen and drain the water. Place a layer of newspaper on the pulp and press out the rest of the water. Turn the screen over while holding the newspaper on it so the newspaper is on the bottom. Carefully lift off the screen. Gently place another layer of newspaper over the pulp and press the water out again. Turn the newspaper over and repeat the pressing with more dry paper. Repeat several times. Gently peel off the new paper and place on dry paper. Dry overnight.

Fun things to try with your papermaking:

- Add 1 tablespoon of laundry starch: this creates a shinier finish on the paper surface.
- Add decorations such as flowers or leaves to your paper pulp as you pour it onto the screen.
- Add food coloring to the pulp mix for colored paper.

Leaf Painting

Collect leaves of different types and vein patterns. Paint an even coat of nontoxic paint on top of a sponge. Place the ribbed side of the leaf on top of the sponge. Place a piece of paper on the leaf and press gently for ten to fifteen seconds. Place the leaf, paint side down, on a piece of paper. Place another piece of paper on top and rub gently for another ten to fifteen seconds. Remove top paper carefully and gently peel off leaf, holding it by its stem.

Torn Paper Art

Save single sheets of colored paper or construction paper that aren't being used. I save flyers that are printed on one side of colored paper. Tear them into small pieces (¼-inch each). Draw a basic outline on a sheet of white paper of what you want to make (such as a Christmas tree, a wreath, a boat, etc.) and glue the torn pieces of paper into the design.

We made a Christmas tree by drawing a triangle for the tree and filling it in with torn green pieces, then adding a few red and blue pieces for ornaments, and a few brown pieces (from a brown paper bag) for the trunk.

Modeling Dough

Kids can help mix this. Add more fun by using rolling pins, potato mashers, and cookie cutters.

1½ C. flour
½ C. salt
food coloring (optional)
½ C. water
¼ C. vegetable oil

In a bowl, mix flour and salt together. To the water, add food coloring, 2 or 3 drops at a time (until desired color is reached), and stir. Slowly add colored water and oil to dough and mix well. Knead dough by hand until soft.

Note: Sprinkle with a little flour and knead in if dough is too sticky. Leftover dough can be stored in plastic bags or airtight containers to keep it soft.

Play Dough

(This is like the above recipe but has a slightly different texture and lasts longer.)

2 C. flour
1 C. salt
4 tsp. cream of tartar
2 C. water with food coloring
2 T. oil

Mix all ingredients together in a pan (nonstick is better). Cook over medium heat until it forms a hard ball, stirring constantly.

As it becomes half-cooked, the dough is hard to mix. Keep stirring until all parts are hardened. Knead to achieve a smooth consistency, This batch of play dough will cost only thirty cents as compared to between two and three dollars for store-bought.

Note: For glitter dough, add glitter when cooking is finished and you are kneading dough.

Try using unsweetened drink mix for the coloring. It also adds fragrance. Use one pack for each recipe.

Edible Modeling Clay

1 C. peanut butter
1 C. nonfat dry milk
⅔ C. powdered sugar
1 C. loose coconut (optional)

Place peanut butter in a large bowl and work in dry milk with fingers. Add powdered sugar and coconut and work in with fingers. The texture should be like play dough. If it's too dry, add more peanut butter. If it's too sticky, add more dry milk. This keeps well in a plastic bag for a week. Try making spiders by rolling a ball for the tummy and one for the head. Use pretzel sticks for the legs and raisins for the eyes.

3-D Salt Map Dough

This is a versatile medium for many projects such as relief maps for school, Christmas ornaments, homemade buttons, and other crafts.

3 C. salt
3 C. flour
2 C. water (approximate)
Poster board, foam board, or thin plywood

Mix salt and flour thoroughly and set aside. Heat the water and add enough to the salt and flour mixture to reach the consistency of frosting. Keep in mind that the more water you use, the longer the dough will take to dry. Draw a picture of what you want to make on a board. Spread the mixture within the boundaries, piling to make a three-dimensional pattern. After the dough dries (one to three days), paint with poster paints.

Aromatic Modeling Dough

This is fun to make at Christmastime. One woman makes it into a piecrust with the top layer latticed and potpourri inside the "pie." Another made ornaments with it by rolling the dough, cutting out shapes, piercing a hole for string or ribbon, and drying them.

¾ C. applesauce
1 C. cinnamon (4 oz.)
1 T. cloves
1 T. nutmeg
2 T. glue

Mix thoroughly and shape into figures (snowmen, bowls, etc.). Lay on cookie sheet and leave in oven overnight with only the oven light on (or at 150° for a few hours).

Painted Pebbles

Gather stones outdoors, looking for unusual shapes and sizes. Paint with acrylic or watercolors. Glue on wobbly eyes to make faces. For a fine finish, apply a coat of clear nail polish when the paint is dry. These make fun gifts for grandparents.

Make a family by hot-gluing several "people" to a piece of driftwood.

Rock Candy

This is fun and teaches patience too.

heat-resistant glass jar
1 C. water
3½ C. sugar
3 10-in. lengths of clean string
pencil

Boil the water in a saucepan. Start adding the sugar a couple of tablespoons at a time. Stir as the sugar dissolves and syrup forms. Keep an eye on the pan at all times so the syrup doesn't boil over. When all the sugar is dissolved and the syrup is clear, remove from the heat and let cool for ten minutes. Pour into glass jar.

Tie one end of each of the lengths of string to the pencil, leaving a space between each one. Rest the pencil over the jar, with the strings lowered into the syrup.

Check the jar daily, but do not disturb. The crystals will form on the strings in about two weeks. If crystals form over the surface, break them up carefully so further evaporation will continue. The candy is "done" whenever you have the amount of crystals you desire. The longer you leave it, the more crystals there will be and the larger they will grow.

Fireworks in January

Color a piece of paper with red, blue, and green crayons (color in large patches of each color). Cover all of the paper. Paint over it with black poster paint or ink. Let it dry. Scratch off firework shapes with a toothpick.

Street Chalk

1 C. plaster of Paris (do not pack)
almost ½ C. cool water
2–3 T. liquid acrylic paint
small paper cups

Pour plaster into a disposable container. Using a disposable stirring stick, stir in most of the water. Add paint and mix well. Add a little more water as the mixture thickens. Stir well and pour into paper cups. Peel off the paper when the chalk is dry.

Juice Lids

Ever wonder what to do with those concentrated juice can lids (the round metal discs with smooth edges)? Here are a few ideas:

- Make refrigerator magnets by gluing small magnets (available by the pack at most craft stores) on the backs and decorating the fronts with the following ideas:
Paint with different colors of fabric glue.
Paint on a thin layer of white glue and cover with sand. Shake off excess. When dry, paste on a cutout camel or other desert animal, or small shells.
Glue on a favorite wallet-sized photo (cut to the size and shape of the lid).
- Create sorting toys for younger children. Save any container

that has a lid (oatmeal box, large yogurt container, etc.) and cut a slit in the lid. Let the little ones put the juice lids in the box one at a time.

Goop

This is much like Gak, found in toy stores, but this recipe will not stain everything it touches, and it washes out of fabrics (unlike the store-bought version). It also makes a great science project because it is the result of a chemical reaction. The homemade version costs about $1.25 versus the store-bought version at $5 to $7.

8 oz. Elmer's glue (use school glue, not Glue-All or washable glue)
¾ C. water, plus food coloring
1 tsp. 20 Mule Team Borax (in most laundry aisles of grocery stores)
½ C. water

In a large bowl, combine the first 2 ingredients until well blended. In a separate cup, combine the Borax and water until the Borax is dissolved. Pour the Borax solution into the glue solution and stir. A large lump will form. Work the lump with your hands, occasionally rubbing into the remaining glue. As you work the lump, the glue will be absorbed, and the lump will become smooth. Store in an airtight plastic box or zippered plastic bag. It will last a few weeks.

Note: If the Goop gets on clothing or fabric, try to wash it before it dries. Spraying with a pretreatment helps. If the Goop dries and hardens before you notice, soak the area overnight, scraping off as much as possible, and then wash in warm water.

Creepy Slime

1 C. cornstarch
½ C. cold water
green food coloring (or other color)

Mix all ingredients in a bowl. Put it in your hand and it slowly creeps. Pound on it on the table and it's solid. Which is it?

Silly Putty

¼ C. liquid laundry starch
¼ C. Elmer's school glue

Mix together. Some have found that mixing inside a plastic bag works best. Store in a plastic container or in the refrigerator. This makes enough for a few kids to each have a glob.

Finger Paint

2 T. cornstarch
2 T. cool water
1 C. boiling water
food coloring

Mix the cool water and cornstarch. Add the boiling water and stir. It should thicken as you stir. When it is cool, divide into small cups or muffin tins. Then add food coloring and mix.

Note: To remove any stains these create, try the stain removal ideas in the next chapter, "Safer and Cheaper."

Quick & Cheap Finger Paint

Mix a few drops of food coloring with some inexpensive shaving cream. The kids can color on paper that is spread on the kitchen table or decorate the bathtub tile. The latter is an easier place to clean up.

MOO-ving Milk

½ C. whole milk
few drops food coloring
few drops liquid detergent

Pour milk into a pie plate or bowl. Drop some food coloring into the milk but don't let the drops touch each other. Add a few drops of detergent and watch the colors swirl. Why is this happening? The detergent is causing the milk fat to separate.

RESOURCES

Cabin Fever Relievers: Hundreds of Games, Activities, and Crafts You Can Use for Creative Indoor Fun, Tina Koch (Redleaf Press, 1997).

Crafts for Kids: A Month-by-Month Idea Book, Barbara L. Dondiego (Tab Books, 1991).

Family Fun Activity Book, Bob Keeshan (Deaconess Press, 1995).

Family Fun Crafts: 500 Creative Activities for You and Your Kids, Deanna F. Cook (Hyperion, 1997).

Incredibly Awesome Crafts for Kids, Sara J. Treinen (Better Homes and Gardens Books, 1992).

Mommy, There's Nothing to Do! Cynthia MacGregor (Replica Books, 2001).

Nature Crafts for Kids—50 Fantastic Things to Make With Mother Nature's Help, Gwen and Terry Krautwurst (Sterling Publishing Co., 1992).

CHAPTER THIRTY

Safer and Cheaper

$ $ $

*S*tore shelves are filled with products we are told we "need" to use in order to effectively clean our homes. Most of them do a great job. But at what price? What's more important to know is that they aren't necessary in order to do a good job of cleaning. I found my great-grandmother's notebook of homemade cleaning recipes. It was inspiring to find alternatives to ready-made cleaning products.

Aside from my interest in being frugal, I began to research alternative cleaners to combat my son's chemical sensitivity. The more I use them, the happier I am at the effect on my pocketbook, my kids, and the environment.

We don't need special cleaning products for each cleaning need. We don't need a special bottle for tile cleaning, and one for the toilet, and another for countertops, floors, or walls. The cleaning supply manufacturers want you to think you need these so they make more money. Many of these products are made from the same ingredients.

There are many good books in the library filled with recipes for cleaners. The following are some of the best recipes I have found—including some from my great-grandmother's notebook.

ALTERNATIVE CLEANING SUPPLIES

Natural cleaners are cheaper. But even though they are natural, they can still cause skin damage. So please wear gloves while cleaning with these substances.

With some basic supplies you can do most of your cleaning. Here is a list of the basic supplies I use and a description of their purpose:

Vinegar

This inexpensive ingredient kills bacteria and mold and can be used as a disinfectant, but without the risk associated with ammonia. Use the distilled type for a less offensive odor. This also can be used to remove soap scum or wash windows, and added to dishwater to make glass sparkle. It can also be used as a stain remover. It has many first-aid uses, such as bee stings, hives, sunburn, gargle for sore throats, and upset stomachs. The chemical name for vinegar is acetic acid.

Baking Soda

This is a versatile, nontoxic cleaner also known as sodium bicarbonate. It can be a nonscratch powder for scrubbing metal and tile surfaces. Diluted in water, it deodorizes and cleans refrigerators, thermoses, etc. Sprinkle on carpets to remove odors. Sprinkle on a grease fire to put out the flame. There are literally hundreds of uses for baking soda.

Borax

This is a natural compound also known as sodium borate. It is a cleaner and a water softener. It can be used to scrub metal and tile surfaces without scratching. It can be poured into drains to keep them clean. It cleans floors well too. It is great for neutralizing the ammonia in urine when soaking diapers. It even kills fleas.

Washing Soda

This is a natural compound that is very versatile. It is also called sodium carbonate (*not* sodium *bi*carbonate). It can be used to freshen laundry and boost laundry detergent. It can also be used to clean bathroom surfaces, greasy stoves, ovens, and grills.

Citrus Peels

Citrus is a fragrant cleaning source. The fruit can be ground up in garbage disposals to freshen and clear out the gunk built up in there. The peels can be boiled and the solution used for cleaning greasy messes, not to mention freshening the air. A manufacturer has bottled this idea in an all-natural solvent called Citra-Solv.

Cleaning Tools

Instead of spending money for scrubbing tools, see what you can reuse around the house. For example, when a toothbrush begins to fray and would normally be discarded, I put it with my cleaning supplies. I use it for cleaning grout and tight spots around faucets. It also cleans jewelry with gemstones very well.

CLEANING RECIPES

Following are my favorite cleaning solutions, which are also simple to make.

Furniture Polish

   1 part lemon juice
   2 parts vegetable or olive oil

Brass Polish

Apply ketchup or Worcestershire sauce. Let stand a few minutes, then rinse. If an area doesn't clean, there must be a buildup of grease or dirt. Clean the residue off with a

The Environmental Cost of Store-Bought Cleaners

The first cost is to people. The chemicals in these cleaners are diluted forms of caustic and dangerous elements. They are washed down the drain. Water treatment plants do not remove chemicals. The effect on us is not entirely known at this time.

The second cost is financial. Most cleaners can be replaced with common household items. These common ingredients cost pennies compared to the dollars the cleaners cost.

The third cost is to the environment. We flush these chemicals down the drain and into the water supply affecting nearby lakes, rivers, plant life, and animals. Municipal water treatment plants don't filter out these chemicals.

paste of salt and vinegar, and then reapply the sauce. Or try a natural product called Citra-Solv, made from citrus peels.

Copper Polish

Coat the surface with ketchup. Let it sit for a few minutes, then rinse off. Rub with a soft cloth to dry.

Silver Polish

Make a paste with ¼ cup baking soda and 1½ T. water. Apply with a damp sponge. Rub, then rinse and buff dry. Or put the baking soda in enough boiling water to cover the silverware. Let sit ten minutes, then polish.

Drain Cleaner

¼ C. baking soda
½ C. vinegar

Pour baking soda in drain. Pour vinegar in drain. Tightly close the drain. Let rest a few minutes. Then flush with boiling water. Repeat until clear. To keep the drain free of buildup, weekly flush with ¼ cup salt, then boiling water.

Hard Water Buildup

Put equal parts vinegar and water inside a teakettle or vase that has mineral buildup. Let sit for at least a half hour. Then scrub out the minerals.

Oven Cleaner

When the spill is still warm, sprinkle with salt and scrub.

Tile and Floor Cleaner

Scrub with a paste of 20 Mule Team Borax and water.

Carpet Cleaner

1 part cornmeal
1 part 20 Mule Team Borax
Combine and sprinkle over carpet. Leave for one hour. Vacuum.

Carpet Odor

Sprinkle baking soda on the carpet and leave overnight. Vacuum well.

Upholstery Cleaner

¼ cup 20 Mule Team Borax
1 T. dishwashing liquid
1 C. warm water
Rub surface with a soft cloth that has been dipped in this solution.

Wall Cleaner

1 gal. hot water
½ C. borax

My Great-Grandma Maggie's Porcelain Cleaner

Rub porcelain with cream of tartar and a damp, soft rag.

Window Cleaner #1

2 C. water
2 T. ammonia

Window Cleaner #2

1 C. vinegar
2 C. water
This does a great job cleaning windows and mirrors.

Toilet Bowl

Sprinkle with baking soda, then pour in a little vinegar. Scrub with a brush. For tougher stains, make a paste of Borax and lemon juice and let it remain on the stain overnight.

General Spot Remover

Dissolve ¼ cup Borax in 2 cups of cold water. Sponge on and let dry. Wash garment or fabric as recommended. This solution works on blood, chocolate, coffee, mildew, and mud.

Ink

Wet the fabric with water, then apply a paste of cream of tartar and lemon juice. Let sit for an hour, then wash as directed. You can also try spraying the garment with hair spray just before washing.

"Washable" Color Markers

Rinse the stain in cold water until it runs clear. Then wet the stain with rubbing alcohol. Blot with another cloth until the color is removed. Wash in hottest water allowed for the fabric.

Poster Paints and Watercolors (on Garments)

Apply rubbing alcohol to the stain and blot with another cloth until no more color comes off. Line dry. If the stain remains, soak garment in one quart of warm water, one teaspoon of dishwashing liquid, and one tablespoon of vinegar. Wash in hottest water temperature the fabric can tolerate.

Poster Paint, Finger Paint, and Watercolors (on Carpeting or Clothing)

First remove as much of the paint as possible by applying a paste of baking soda and water to the stain. When the paste is dry, vacuum the spot. To remove what remains, soak a sponge in rubbing alcohol and blot the stain until no more color comes off on the sponge (I stand on my sponge to encourage the paint to soak up). If some stain still remains, blot again with a sponge soaked in ammonia.

Silly Putty on Carpeting or Garments

My mom says that when I left Silly Putty on the carpet, she froze it by applying ice. It became brittle and peeled right off.

Chewing Gum in Hair

Slather peanut butter on the gum. It will dissolve it. Then comb it out. Keep doing this until all gum is removed. You can also try freezing it as with the Silly Putty above.

Play Dough on Carpeting

Remove larger pieces while dough is still pliable. Let the rest dry overnight into the carpet. Make a solution of warm water with some dishwashing liquid. Use a stiff brush dipped in the water to work the rest of the dough out.

Lipstick

Rub with shortening (not margarine—this has yellow dye in it) and clean with washing soda.

PERSONAL CLEANSING AND COMFORT

Bath Time

For a soothing bath, add one cup of dry milk to the bath water. For soft skin, add one cup of baking soda as well.

Toothpaste

8 T. baking soda
3 T. glycerin (available at drugstores)
1–2 tsp. flavoring (peppermint, orange, etc.)

Blend well and store in airtight container. For a simpler and quick paste: Mix equal parts baking soda and salt. For flavor, add a dash of cinnamon, mint extract, or flavored fluoride liquid.

Cleansing Cream

3 T. coconut oil
1 T. vegetable oil
1 T. glycerin (available at drugstores)
2 tsp. water

Melt these on low heat. Remove from heat and beat with a whisk or fork until well blended. Store in airtight jar. If your house becomes very hot, keep the cream in the refrigerator.

Astringent

Below are three ways to make astringent. My favorite is the first. It is very refreshing.

Mix equal parts witch hazel and water,
    or
Mix equal parts distilled white vinegar and water,
    or
Mash some strawberries—rub them on your face. Rinse with warm water.

Bee Stings/Sunburn/Hives

Vinegar can instantly relieve the pain and itch of bee stings, hives, or sunburn—much faster than a baking soda paste. Soak brown paper (from a paper bag) with vinegar and apply to the affected area.

Antacid

½ tsp. baking soda
½ C. water

For an upset stomach, combine and drink.

Cuts and Burns

Thoroughly clean an injury—and keep it clean—and you should fare well. Avoid remedies such as iodine, hydrogen peroxide, Merthiolate, Mercurochrome, Bactine, or Campho-Phenique. These damage the skin and can lead to worse scarring.

Ice Bag

2 quart-sized resealable plastic bags
1 C. water
½ C. rubbing alcohol

Put liquid in one bag and seal tightly. Put the other bag around it and seal it for double protection. Freeze. It will be slushy so it can mold to the wound or swollen area. Place on the skin for ten to twenty minutes.

Note: Wrap with a cloth if skin is sensitive to the cold. Beware of causing frostbite to the area.

My Great-Grandma Maggie's Remedy for Arthritis Pain

Mix rubbing alcohol with a few drops of wintergreen and rub on the affected parts.

Athlete's Foot

½ C. apple cider vinegar
2 C. hot water

Soak your feet in the solution until it cools. Do this once a day for about a week. It should kill the fungi.

Skin Irritations

For relief of minor burns, itches from insect bites, sunburn, and poison oak or ivy, smooth on the fresh juice of the aloe plant. Keep a plant in the house and break off a leaf, releasing the juices inside. Apply directly to the affected area as often as needed.

Yeast Infections

The live yogurt culture, acidophilus, when eaten, is helpful in combating yeast infection.

$\mathcal{M}$ISCELLANEOUS REMEDIES

My Great-Grandma Maggie's Remedy for No-Run Stockings

Soak stockings in a mixture of alum (used to make pickles) and water to prevent running.

Garden Pesticide #1

1 T. dishwashing detergent
1 C. vegetable oil
Mix and store in an airtight container. When needed, mix 1–2 T. solution with 1 C. water.
Spray on plants, covering all leaf and stem surfaces. (from the U.S. Department of Agriculture)

Garden Pesticide #2

3 onions
2 quarts water
4 cloves garlic
Boil these together for an hour. Discard onions and garlic. When liquid is cool, place in a spray bottle and spray on plants.

Snail Bait

2 tsp. sugar
½ tsp. yeast
2 C. water
Mix in a shallow dish or pie pan. Snails are attracted to this bait, and will drown in it.

Weeds

To kill unwanted growth in your garden, pour boiling water directly on weeds. To save plants around the weeds, water good plants and surrounding soil well just before applying the hot water. This cools the plants, and if any hot water seeps onto the

good plants, the water already in the soil will cool it down. Make
sure you pour the hot water only on the weed.

RESOURCES

Better Basics for the Home: Simple Solutions for Less-Toxic Living, Annie
   Berthold-Bond (Three Rivers Press, 1999).

Bug Busters: Poison-Free Pest Controls for Your House & Garden, Bern-
   ice Lifton (Avery Publishing, 1991).

*Clean House, Clean Planet: Clean Your House for Pennies a Day, the
   Safe, Nontoxic Way*, Karen N. Logan (Pocket Books, 1997).

Clean Your House Safely and Effectively Without Harmful Chemicals,
   Randy Dunford (Magni Company, 1993).

*Creating a Healthy Household: The Ultimate Guide for Healthier, Safer,
   Less-Toxic Living*, Lynn M. Bower (Healthy House Institute,
   2000).

*The Green Kitchen Handbook: Practical Advice, References, and Sources
   for Transforming the Center of Your Home Into a Healthy, Livable
   Place*, Annie Berthold-Bond (HarperCollins, 1997).

*Home Safe Home: Protecting Yourself and Your Family From Everyday
   Toxins and Harmful Household Products in the Home*, Debra L.
   Dadd (Jeremy P. Tarcher, 1997).

CHAPTER THIRTY-ONE

An Easy $10,000

$ $ $

*I*t is amazing how a few small changes can add up to large savings. Throughout this book, I have tried to demonstrate this fact. Each savings idea can save you some money. The more ideas you adopt, the more money you will save.

This last chapter is a quick summary of a few easy ways to save. Each idea has a potential savings value next to it. If you applied all of these ideas, they could add up to an annual savings of $10,000. (This assumes you haven't already been applying them.) Your savings may vary from the potential listed. Some of these ideas are discussed in previous chapters in more depth. I am including them in this list in case this is the only chapter you read!

ELECTRICITY

$100   Enroll in load management programs and off-hour-rate programs offered by your utility company.

$100   Turn your furnace down by three degrees (lowering one degree saves 3 percent).

$30   Lower the temperature on your hot water heater to between 110° and 120°. It's not necessary to have it any hotter and it wastes energy.

$20   Run your dishwasher only when you have a full load.

$20   Let the dishes air-dry instead of using the heat cycle.

$20   Wash your laundry in cold water.

$\mathscr{L}$ONG-DISTANCE SERVICE

$60   Switch to a no-fee service.

$100   Compare the per-minute rates.

$100   Call during off-peak hours.

$100   Use e-mail instead of telephoning.

$100   Use free Internet dialing (e.g., *www.Dialpad.com*).

$\mathscr{A}$UTOMOBILE USE

$100   Keep your engine tuned and your tires inflated to their proper pressure.

$100   Get the junk out of your trunk. The more weight an engine has to pull, the more gas it uses. Every extra 250 pounds your engine hauls, your car consumes an extra mile per gallon of gas.

$100   Fill up the gas tank when near a gas station with low prices.

$\mathscr{C}$HECKING ACCOUNT

$100   Choose a checking account with no fees (usually requires a minimum balance).

$50   Have your payroll checks automatically deposited to reduce your monthly bank fees.

$100   Use your own bank's ATM to avoid usage fees.

$\mathscr{C}$REDIT CARDS

$200   Compare annual percentage rates (APR) and switch to a card with a lower rate.

$100   Combine all of the cards you use (gas, department store, etc.) into one or two cards and avoid late payment and over-the-credit-limit fees.

$\mathscr{I}$NSURANCE

$400   Compare rates with other companies in your area.

$100   Reduce or drop comprehensive and/or collision coverage on old cars.

$100   Increase your deductibles.

$100   Get a multipolicy discount by keeping all insurance policies with one company.

$100   Get as many discounts as you can: nonsmoker, low-mileage, antitheft device, good student, senior citizen, military, etc.

BABY CARE

$500   Make your own baby food.

ENTERTAINMENT

$2,000   Reduce how often you eat out by 50 percent.

$150   Limit video rentals and use library videos instead.

$600   Don't go to the mall for entertainment. The more time you spend there, the more you spend.

$250   Reduce your cable service: eliminate movie channels and step down to minimum service.

$400   If you have movie channels, stop renting videos.

CLOTHES

$700   Plan your clothing needs and buy your clothes at thrift and consignment stores.

VACATIONS

$3,000   Visit friends and relatives instead of amusement parks. Drive instead of fly. Visit local attractions instead of cross-country locales. Take a cooler of food and refill at grocery stores instead of eating out at each meal. Use motels that provide a free meal for kids or where kids stay free.

Menu Plans

*U*sing the following menus, it is possible to feed a family of four for about $65 per week. All of these meals are what we eat. They are frugal if made from scratch. Repeat some meals if you can. Some of the recipes for these are found in chapter 15. Many more will be featured in my new cookbook, *Miserly Meals.*

Breakfast

Homemade granola
Homemade cinnamon rolls
Muffins
Hot cereal (oatmeal or cream of wheat)
Pancakes, French toast, or waffles with homemade pancake syrup

Lunches

Peanut butter and jelly sandwiches
Chicken salad sandwiches (made with leftover chicken)
Lunchmeat sandwiches
Hot dogs
Tuna sandwiches
Cheese and crackers
Macaroni and cheese
Soup and crackers
Homemade burgers

Bagels & cream cheese
Leftovers

Snacks & Fruits

Homemade cookies and granola bars
Homemade banana bread
Popcorn (caramel, spiced, plain)
Rice pudding
Salads
Fresh vegetables
Homemade fruit leather

Drinks

Juices, milk, or water

Dinners

Thai Noodle Meal
Spaghetti with meatballs
Vegetarian spaghetti (grated vegetables instead of meat)
Chicken and potatoes with cream of mushroom soup sauce
Beans and rice
Fajitas
Homemade veggie burgers
Minestrone soup
Enchilada casserole (tortillas, beans, cheese, and enchilada
    sauce)
Potpies
Stir-fry (using leftover meat)
Burritos
Lentil rice casserole
Quiche
Vegetable patties
Pesto
Leftover bread meal
Leek & Potato Soup
Anne's Squash Casserole

Black Bean Soup
Huevos Rancheros
Leftover chicken Italian meal
Leftovers smorgasbord
Baked potato smorgasbord
Vegetarian chili and homemade cornbread
Easy Microwave Lasagna
Messy Chicken
Indian Curry
Chinese Pineapple Chicken
Pizza
Poor Man's Steak

Substitutions, Equivalency Table, and Metric Conversion

Substitutions

Dairy

3 oz. cream cheese	= 6 T. cream cheese
4 oz. bleu cheese	= 1 C. crumbled bleu cheese
4 oz. hard cheese	= 1 C. shredded Cheddar or Swiss
4 oz. soft cheese	= 1¼ C. shredded Monterey jack or American
2 C. whipped cream	= 1 C. heavy cream
2 egg yolks	= 1 whole egg
1 C. sour milk	= 1 T. lemon juice or vinegar plus 1 C. milk
1 C. buttermilk	= 1 C. yogurt

Chocolate

1 sq. unsweetened chocolate	= 3 T. cocoa plus 1 T. butter
1 oz. chocolate	= 1 sq. chocolate
1 sq. chocolate	= 4 T. grated chocolate
1 lb. cocoa	= 4 C. cocoa

Nuts

1 lb. almonds in shells	= 1¼ C. almond meat
1 lb. pecans in shells	= 2¼ C. chopped pecans

1 lb. walnut in shells	= 1½ C. walnut meat
1 lb. peanuts in shells	= 2¼ C. peanuts

Pasta and Breads

1 C. uncooked rice	= 3 C. cooked rice
¼ lb. uncooked pasta	= 2 C. cooked pasta
1 C. fine crumbs	= 4 slices bread or 28 unsalted crackers or 14 graham cracker sq.
Bread crumbs	= dry pancake mix (when desperate)
1 C. bread cubes	= 2 slices bread
1 lb. oats	= 2⅔ C. oats
Main dish piecrust	= pan lined with mashed canned beans, mashed potatoes, cooked rice, or noodles

Baking/Spices

1 tsp. baking powder	= ¼ tsp. baking soda + ½ tsp. cream of tartar
1 C. cake flour	= 1 C. all-purpose flour + 2 T. cornstarch
1 C. self-rising flour	= 1 C. flour + 1½ tsp. baking powder + ½ tsp. salt
1 pkg. dry yeast	= 2 tsp. dry yeast
2 C. corn syrup	= 1 C. sugar
1 C. honey	= 1¼ C. sugar
1 C. molasses	= ¾ C. sugar
1¼ C. confectioners' sugar	= 1 C. granulated sugar
1 T. instant minced onion (rehydrated)	= 1 small fresh onion
1 T. prepared mustard	= 1 tsp. dry mustard
⅛ tsp. garlic powder	= 1 small clove garlic
2 T. flour	= 1 T. cornstarch as a thickening agent
1½ C. Ketchup	= 1 C. tomato sauce plus ½ C. sugar and 2 T. vinegar

1 tsp. dried herbs	= 1 T. fresh herbs
1 pkg. (2 tsp.) active dry yeast	= 1 cake compressed yeast
1 lb. box of these sugars	= 2 C. white sugar, 2¼ C. brown sugar, or 3½ C. confectioners' sugar
2 C. butter	= 1 lb. butter
8–10 egg whites	= 1 C. egg whites
12–14 yolks	= 1 C. egg yolks

Fruits

1 C. sliced apple	= 1 large apple
1½ C. mashed banana	= 3 bananas or 2 C. sliced bananas
2–3 T. lemon juice	= 1 lemon
1–2 T. lime juice	= 1 lime
3½ C. berries	= 1 qt. berries
3 C. dried apricots	= 1 lb. dried apricots
2¾ C. raisins	= 1 lb. raisins

Vegetables and Legumes

1 C. chopped celery	= 2 stalks celery
½ C. chopped onion	= 1 medium-sized onion
1¼ C. mashed potatoes	= 3 potatoes
2 C. mashed potatoes	= 1 lb. raw potatoes
1 lb. dried beans	= 6–9 C. cooked
1 C. canned tomatoes	= 1⅓ C. cut fresh tomatoes
1 lb. fresh tomatoes	= 1½ C. chopped tomatoes

Equivalency Table

dash	= less than ⅛ tsp.
3 tsp.	= 1 T.
4 T.	= ¼ C.
8 T.	= ½ C.
8 T.	= 4 oz.

16 T.	= 1 C.
⅞ C.	= ¾ C. + 2 T.
1 T.	= ½ fl. oz.
8 oz. can or jar	= 1 C.
10½ oz. can	= 1¼ C.
12 oz. can tuna	= 1½ C. tuna
2½ lb. can	= 3½ C.
15 oz. can	= 1⅓ C.
8 qt. (dry)	= 1 peck
4 pecks	= 1 bushel
16 oz. (dry)	= 1 lb.

METRIC CONVERSION CHART

1 gr.	= .035 oz.
1 kg.	= 2.21 lbs.
1 oz.	= 29 gr.
1 tsp.	= 5 mil.
1 T.	= 15 mil.
1 C.	= 237 mil.
1 lb.	= 454 gr.
1 liter	= 1.056 liquid qt. or 1000 mil.
1 qt.	= 0.946 liters

COST BREAKDOWNS
(based on sale prices)

1 C. flour	= 5¢
1 egg	= 9¢
½ C. butter	= 25¢
1 C. sugar	= 18¢
1 apple	= 7¢

Additional Resources

*H*ere are some very good resources for learning more about how to live on less. Some chapters have their own resource section with applicable books. These are in addition to those.

MISERLY LIVING

Brennen, Sherri. *Better Living: Tips for Saving Time and Money*. WVEC-TV Inc., 1994.

Dacyczyn, Amy. *The Complete Tightwad Gazette: Promoting Thrift As a Viable Alternative Lifestyle*. Villard Books, 1999.

Dappen, Andy. *Cheap Tricks: 100s of Ways You Can Save 1000s of Dollars*. Brier Books, 1992.

Editors of Rodale. *Cut Your Spending in Half Without Settling for Less*. Rodale Press, 1995.

Ellis, Gwen, and Jo Ann Janssen. *Decorating on a Shoestring*. Broadman Holman, 1999.

Gallagher, Patricia. *Raising Happy Kids on a Reasonable Budget*. Better Way Books, 1993.

Gorman, Charlotte. *The Frugal Mind: 1,483 Money-Saving Tips for Surviving the New Millennium*. Nottingham Books, 1998.

Hunt, Mary. *The Best of the Cheapskate Monthly: Simple Tips for Living Lean in the '90s*. St. Martin's Paperbacks, 1993.

Lesko, Matthew. *Free Stuff for Busy Moms*. Information U.S.A., Inc., 1999.

McBride, Tracey. *Frugal Luxuries: Simple Pleasures to Enhance Your Life and Comfort Your Soul*. Bantam Books, 1997.

McCoy, Jonni. *Frugal Families: Making the Most of Your Hard-Earned Money*. Full Quart Press, 1998.

Miller, Mark W. *The Complete Idiot's Guide to Being a Cheapskate*. Macmillan, 1998.

Moore, Melodie. *The Frugal Almanac: Over 500 Money-Saving Ideas*. NAL, 1997.

Paris, James L. *Absolutely Amazing Ways to Save Money on Everything*. Harvest House, 1999.

Roberts, William. *How to Save Money on Just About Everything*. Paladin Press, 1996.

Roth, Larry. *The Best of Living Cheap News: Practical Advice on Saving Money and Living Well*. NTC Publishing Group, 1996.

Simmons, Lee and Barbara. *Penny-Pinching: How to Lower Your Everyday Expenses Without Lowering Your Standard of Living*. Bantam Books, 1999.

Taylor-Hough, Deborah. *A Simple Choice: A Practical Guide for Saving Your Time, Money, and Sanity*. Champion Books, 2000.

Yates, Cynthia. *The Complete Guide to Creative Gift Giving*. Servant Publications, 1997.

Yorkey, Mike. *21 Days to a Thrifty Lifestyle*. Zondervan, 1997.

FAMILY BUDGETING AND SAVINGS

Briles, Judith. *10 Smart Money Moves for Women: How to Conquer Your Financial Fears*. NTC, 1999.

Burkett, Larry. *Your Complete Guide to Financial Security*. Budget Book Service, 1998.

Chilton, David. *The Wealthy Barber: Everyone's Commonsense Guide to Becoming Financially Independent*. Prima Publishing, 1998.

Detweiler, Gerri, Marc Eisenson, and Nancy Castleman. *Invest in Yourself: Six Secrets to a Rich Life*. John Wiley & Sons, 1998.

Humber, Wilson J. *Dollars and Sense: Making the Most of What You Have*. Navpress, 1993.

O'Neill, Barbara. *Saving on a Shoestring: How to Cut Expenses, Reduce Debt, Stash More Cash*. Dearborn Financial Publishing, Inc., 1995.

Pond, Jonathan. *The New Century Family Money Book*. Dell Hardcover, 1993.

Savage, Terry. *Terry Savage's New Money: Strategies for the '90s.* Harper Business, 1994.

Scott, David. *The Guide to Personal Budgeting: How to Stretch Your Dollars Through Wise Money Management.* Globe Pequot, 1995.

Wall, Ginita. *The Way to Save: A 10-Step Blueprint for Lifetime Security.* Henry Holt and Co., 1993.

GETTING OUT OF DEBT AND BEING FINANCIALLY FREE

Blue, Ron. *Taming the Money Monster: Five Steps to Conquering Debt.* Focus on the Family Publishing, 1993.

Brunette, William K. *Conquer Your Debt.* Prentice Hall Press, 1990.

Detweiler, Gerri, Marc Eisenson, and Nancy Castleman. *Slash Your Debt.* Financial Literacy Center, 1999.

Hunt, Mary. *The Cheapskate Monthly Money Makeover.* St. Martin's Paperbacks, 1995.

Paris, James L. *Living Financially Free.* Harvest House Publishers, 1994.

STARTING A HOME BUSINESS

Brabec, Barbara. *Homemade Money—How to Select, Start, Manage, Market and Multiply the Profits of a Business at Home.* Better Way Books, 1997.

Demas, Cheryl. *The Work-at-Home Mom's Guide to Home Business: Stay at Home and Make Money With Wahm.Com.* Hazen Publishers, Inc., 2000.

Folger, Liz. *The Stay-at-Home Mom's Guide to Making Money: How to Create the Business That's Right for You, Using the Skills and Interests You Already Have.* Prima Publishing, 2000.

Gwen, Ellis. *101 Ways to Make Money at Home.* Vine Books, 1996.

Huff, Priscilla Y. *101 Best Home-Based Businesses for Women.* Prima Publishing, 1998.

Hull, Caroline, and Tanya Wallace. *Moneymaking Moms: How Work at Home Can Work for You.* Citadel Press, 1998.

Levinson, Jay. *555 Ways to Earn Extra Money.* Henry Holt, 1991.

Oberlin, Loriann H. *Working at Home While the Kids Are There Too.* Career Press, 1997.

Parlapiano, Ellen H. *Mompreneurs: A Mother's Practical Step-by-Step Guide to Work-at-Home Success.* Berkley Publishing Group, 1996.

Partow, Donna. *Homemade Business: A Woman's Step-by-Step Guide to Earning Money at Home.* Focus on the Family Publishing, 1999.

Roberts, Lisa M. *How to Raise a Family and a Career Under One Roof: A Parent's Guide to Home Business.* Bookhaven Press, 1997.

Sanders, Darcie, and Martha Bullen. *Turn Your Talents Into Profits: 100+ Terrific Ideas for Starting Your Own Home-Based Microbusiness.* Simon & Schuster, 1998.